Effective Integration
Physically Handicapped Children in
Primary Schools

Sylvia B. Howarth

NFER-NELSON

Published by The NFER-NELSON Publishing Company Ltd.,
Darville House, 2 Oxford Road East,
Windsor, Berkshire SL4 1DF, England

and in the United States of America by
NFER-NELSON, 242 Cherry Street, Philadelphia, PA 19106–1906.
Tel: (215) 238 0939. Telex: 244489

First Published 1987
© 1987, Sylvia B. Howarth

Library of Congress Cataloging in Publication data

Howarth, Sylvia B.
  Effective Integration.

  Bibliography: p.
  includes index.
  1. Handicapped children–Education (elementary – Great Britain. 2.
Mainstreaming in education–Great Britain, I. Title. II. Title: Physically
Handicapped Children in Primary Schools. DNLM: 1. Education, Special–United
States. 2. Handicapped.
LC 4231 H832E LC4036.G7H64   1987   371.9'0941   86–28539
ISBN 0-7005-1135-0

Typesetting by First Page Ltd, Watford, England
Printed and bound in Great Britain
by Billing & Sons Limited, Worcester.

ISBN 0 7005 1135 0
Code 8279 02 1

To my parents, May and Harry Howarth
with love and gratitude,
the pupils of John Chilton School (1977–1981)
and their parents,
who shared my belief in the concept of integration,
and who afforded me the opportunity of putting
integration into action,
and in memory of Ahmed, Fiona and David.

The doctors believe I have a disease
called muscular dystrophy. Whatever it is,
I've got it and have to live with it,
which I accept, and will do my utmost to
lead my life as normally as I can.
I first went to a special school. I was
very happy but they couldn't really give
me the education I required. I am quite
lucky in that I am reasonably academically
clever. It was decided that I should go full
time to an ordinary high school. The first
year was hard for both me, the teachers and
my fellow pupils. It has all turned out well.
I have made many friends, although they were
amazed and confused to begin with.
I have been allowed a great opportunity and
I must show other people that the idea of
handicapped people going into an ordinary
school can work. I must pave the way for
more children to follow in my tracks.
Really the past is no good to me any more.
It's the future that's my challenge, as
it is to all handicapped persons.
I don't think because a person is physically
handicapped they should be treated
differently. We can be useful to the human
society and I personally am going to be.
I like being me, it's a challenge!

Mark O'Shaughnessy
Pupil of John Chilton School (1977–1982)

Contents

Part IV: Policy Implications

List of Tables

List of Appendices

Foreword

The integration of children with significant disabilities or handi-caps into mainstream schools is for some a matter of human rights. Others see it as an ideological movement which is prepared to sacrifice individual children upon the altar of an abstract principle. The majority of the professionals and parents involved occupy the middle ground, where simplistic pictures in black and white give way to the light and shade of what is often a very complex issue.

The Warnock Committee was wise to remind us in 1978 that most children with disabilities are and always have been in mainstream schools since the beginning of universal education. This is the group which is popularly referred to now as 'the 18 per cent'. The smaller group with more severe problems ('the 2 per cent'), most of whom merit a 'statement' of need under the 1981 Education Act, have thus become the main focus of interest and of concern in the context of moves to achieve greater integration following implementation of the Act. However, lest we should forget the historical context prior to Warnock, it is interesting to recall that official government policy as far back as 1944 was that 'no handicapped child should be sent to a special school who can be satisfactorily educated in an ordinary school'.

This very welcome book by Sylvia Howarth concentrates mostly on children with significant or severe physical disabilities or conditions, who are in primary schools. The empirical evidence which forms the heart of the book is based upon a detailed study of 50 such handicapped children in nine schools. The author is careful to point out the dangers of too slavish generalizations from a relatively small sample. However, the findings, drawn from interviews, questionnaires and tests, are fascinating. They confirm and reinforce views which many practitioners in the field will recognize, but from time to time her results challenge and question prevailing wisdom.

The final section dealing with policy implications is a perceptive and valuable discussion of the issues illuminated by the findings. It embraces all the vital ingredients of effective integration, e.g. adequate resources, including appropriate staffing ratios and good support services to schools and to parents; positive attitudes on the part of staff in the mainstream school, which can be fostered by the right preparatory work and consultations with the whole staff; interdisciplinary co-operation; and parental involvement. A point which I was particularly pleased to see Sylvia Howarth emphasizing is one which is often missed in discussions on this issue, namely the value to the entire school when the successful integration of handicapped children is achieved. This is not merely reflected in the attitudes towards handicap by non-handicapped pupils and by staff but by an increased sensitivity to the special needs of all children.

Ronald Davie

Part I

Integration

1
Integration in Practice

Attitudes towards the concept of integration

The attitudes of professional persons concerned with the placement of a handicapped child in a system of integrated education play an important role in establishing firm foundations on which other professionals concerned with meeting the special needs of pupils can build. A positive attitude from those professionals involved with the handicapped child and concerned with his care, treatment and education, fused with a realistic parental attitude towards achievement and expectation, can effectively set the pace for the realization of the child's full potential within the mainstream school system.

Preparation for integration is of paramount importance, and this requires extensive support from all the professional services involved with the handicapped child from birth. The most important recipients of such support are the family and their child and, at a later stage, the school, the staff and the non-handicapped pupils. Let us establish a criteria for integration. Not only should the school be carefully selected, but also the physically handicapped child and his family, to ensure uniformity of attitude and expectation. For example, a child with special needs requiring specialized equipment and resources would be more realistically placed in a school where there was an attitude which resulted in a practical rather than a formal academic approach to education. Staff should be willing to accept handicapped children, and show a sympathy for, and an understanding of, the handicaps and associated problems. They also need to adopt helpful and constructive attitudes, and aim to be of one mind, as far as integration is concerned.

Warnock (1978) stressed that teachers should have the fullest information about any handicapped child who was to join their class. They should discuss and plan the child's education with their colleagues before the child joins the school. Parents should be fully involved in preparations and encouraged in the attitude that their acceptance of the child will influence his or her acceptance by the whole family – both important prerequisites for the child's successful integration. Similarly, parents need to be closely involved in the assessment of their child's special needs, and their active co-operation with all those involved in meeting the child's special needs encouraged.

The level of supportive services is of equal importance, given that such support can promote positive thinking, and develop constructive attitudes towards handicap. Have schools the right to look to Child and Family Guidance Services for assistance in meeting special educational needs? Would more mainstream schools accept more handicapped pupils if greater thought could be given to pupil selection; to the creation of a co-ordinated, well-staffed network of support services, and to the rethinking and adaptation of the curriculum. The handicapped child is an asset to the mainstream school if, ideally, he brings with him a supportive team to assist and meet the educational development needs of his non-handicapped peers.

Obvious practical difficulties imposed by a physical disability must not be allowed to neglect the important repercussions of a defect upon the child's whole psychological development (Wall, 1979). The attitudes of those professionals who are involved closely with the handicapped child in his first few years, and with his parents, must not allow negative thought to override the importance of constructive and highly stimulating planning, which will ensure vital growth in emotional and intellectual development. This is necessary to ensure that as the handicapped child becomes aware of his difference from others, his personality development will not deviate. If his handicap is not accepted the child may develop a guilt complex, and view his handicap as a punishment, or turn aggressive against his environment, because of fear and anxiety. In contrast, over-protective attitudes may well result in physically handicapped children finding refuge in their disability, and failing to achieve and perform to their maximum potential. An over-sympathetic and compassionate attitude on the part of the teacher may lead to a lowering of expectations and standards, and the acceptance of minimal educational performance. The teacher's reaction to the child will be reflected in his reaction to his handicap. Behavioural tendencies of rejection or over protection will hinder the child in his psychological development, and hinder parents from accepting the child as he is. Negative parental attitudes can affect total family adjustment, can cause adverse reactions among siblings, and possibly result in the handicapped child being at the centre of marital conflict.

However, the problem of parent guidance is complicated, and far too frequently there is a lack of understanding by medical, social and educational services. A lack of liaison and failure to co-operate, may ultimately be prejudicial to the handicapped child's pattern of adjustment, and his ability to cope. A positive attitude can be established, if all the services involved with the child give full co-operation in the first instance to the parents, and secondly to those involved with providing the handicapped child with an education suitable to his needs. Social class differences may reflect in attitudes towards the child with a handicap, and this may influence placement in school. Different cultural backgrounds place different emphasis on expectations of the child; family size affects both the child's behaviour and his ability to interact socially and parental attitudes and expectations influence educational achievements.

The influence of perception and attitude towards special provision and integrated schooling

Garnett (1976) wrote that one of the main factors helping integration was the encouraging and understanding attitudes of school staff, with headteachers and senior staff who were particularly aware of the children's needs, wanting to be actively involved. Since an increasing proportion of handicapped children, at present in special schools will be educated in mainstream schools, adequate specialist training for teachers with responsibility for children with special needs is, in itself, a special need. The classroom teacher has the responsibility for the education of most children with special educational needs and successful integration is really dependent upon flexible and helpful attitudes amongst the teachers and within the LEA.

The headteacher's supportive role is of great importance. Primarily, he should exercise oversight of the special educational provision in response to the identification of the special needs of his pupils. He will be required to work closely with outside education and support services, collaborating with special school headteacher colleagues, and maintaining a close liaison with the special education adviser and other LEA officers with responsibility for special education. Ideally, the perception and attitudes of both staff working with children with special needs, and the headteacher, who is trained to give guidance, is aware of the importance of co-operation, and is in a position to act as a co-ordinator, will greatly influence the success of integrated provision (Howarth, 1979).

But what of those teachers and parents who are unable to overcome emotional and psychological reactions aroused by the handicapping conditions? Other teachers may have difficulty in normal class control and in dealing with stresses caused by extremes of deviation, without the added responsibility of a severely handicapped child. The social role of illness can have an extreme effect on education and adjustment and the non-handicapped can project deep feelings of inadequacy onto the handicapped, and regard them with fear and anxiety – the roots of prejudice. Society is permissive in times of illness and this factor can release the child from obligations in the learning situation, thus further handicapping him by not demanding full use of potential. Hence, generally low academic standards of physically handicapped pupils are explained, or attempted to be, by refer-ence to low intelligence, by lack of special facilities or by frequent absences from school. Is this the real reason behind the argument against integration? Any condition, however mild or serious, becomes more or less severely handicapping according to how far those involved closely with the child – family, school, medical and social workers – perceive the meaning of the handicap to the child. A positive attitude must be adopted, to ensure that essential emotional, social and conceptual experiences which underlie successful learning, are provided in spite of disability, to enhance the success of integrated schooling.

The undoubted acceptance of the concept of special needs is probably assisted by the assumption that there is an accurate process of assessment which will correctly examine children and define their needs. What is needed is for the school to adapt its programmes to meet the individual needs of the child, to promote a shift of emphasis from a focus on handicapping conditions and problems, to a focus on learning needs, which will more positively influence perception and attitudes towards special provision in integrated learning situations.

Chazan *et al* (1980) point out that certain factors play an important part in the teacher's handling of children with special needs, namely the teacher's general attitude to her role in the classroom; the extent to which her training has helped increase her perception of the children's difficulties, and the effect of classroom conditions on promoting or hampering integration. According to Hegarty and Pocklington (1981) 'it is worth noting that integration programmes almost by definition entail a dispersal of staff, pupils and resources'. This has implications for training and staff development, yet the concentration of expertise, resources, and pupils with special needs provides a stimulating environment as well as an experimental situation, where alternative approaches to particular problems can be tried out and evaluated. In the long term, the aim must be the extensive promotion of initial and early in-service training, for the majority of teachers who are likely to encounter pupils with special educational needs.

Hegarty and Pocklington (1981) discovered that there was a striking degree of acceptance on the part of mainstream teachers: 90 per cent of all respondents felt that the placement of handicapped pupils at their school was appropriate. This book identifies an equally encouraging degree of acceptance. Pupils reflect teacher attitudes and direct contact is regarded as the most effective method of improving attitudes amongst pupils. After a period of initial curiosity, especially in the case of very young children with physical handicaps, the presence of pupils with special needs is accepted as a matter of course; rejection or mere tolerance is uncommon.

Socialization and behaviour

The philosophy of integration advocates the 'right of all children to acceptance within school programmes regardless of how they may deviate from "norm" in appearance, performance or behaviour' (Meisgeier, 1976). A physically handicapped child soon learns to cope with the relative narrowness and familiarity of the physical environment, and its obvious permanence, if he is given suitable independence training and encouragement. The child's personal and social experiences need to be fully developed; shortcomings in such areas of experience are frequently reflected in low social adaptation levels and, consequently, in social and behavioural adjustment.

Is severity of handicap directly related to problems of emotional development and social adjustment? A severe disability can often permit better social and emotional adjustment than a mild disability. The child with a severe physical handicap is so obviously disabled that he need make no excuse for his handicap, nor strive to conceal it, and attempt to act 'normally'. More important than the degree of handicap, is the extent of the limitations imposed by the handicap.

To what extent does a disability cause greater dependency upon others? How the child reacts to this dependency and how much it is acknowledged by those who deal with him will give a measure of the child's handicap in functional terms. This introduces aspects of social development and emotional reaction, and indicates the need for the child to be viewed as part of his social environment, and to be assessed reacting within that environment. Perhaps the terms disability and handicap are judgemental and dependent upon implied social values. Is there a necessary relationship between physique and behaviour, or is behaviour a function of a person interacting with his environment?

The majority of children who are handicapped, however, do not deviate physically or physiologically from the normal in any marked way. Their learning problems appear to arise from some imbalance between their power to adjust and learn, and an environment which is in some way deficient or, at least, discrepant from their needs. Can we assume that it is possible to manipulate the environment so that function will be improved over time? Will suitable environmental help enable all children to achieve some standard of normality or be restored to a fullness of learning, capable of being achieved without handicap? Can the environment be the reason for all deficiencies in a child's learning or adjustment?

A primary goal of integration is to facilitate contact between pupils with special educational needs and their non-handicapped peers. Integration permits many opportunities for legitimate social contact during lessons, and so specific intervention to promote interaction is both necessary and effective. Gottlieb (1979) suggested that merely placing the handicapped and non-handicapped together does not of itself increase the latter's willingness to accept the former socially. A successful ploy has been to use non-handicapped peers as helpers to assist in the development of social skills and play skills, and a later chapter describes some of the benefits of peer-tutoring.

Hegarty and Pocklington (1981) found in the UK a widespread belief in the efficacy of locational integration to extend beyond itself and lead to a degree of social integration. Rose (1979) implemented a formal intervention programme in one school, based on the notion of peer-tutoring, which enabled non-handicapped pupils to assist those with difficulties. This formal intervention was geared to pupils with moderate to severe learning difficulties, and Rose's conclusion was that 'the programme demonstrated, in a very short period, the ease with which attitudes can change provided guidelines are established'. So we can assume that a realistic programme is essential to enable the handicapped child to identify with other handicapped children and to achieve security and independence. This will increase their ability to tolerate a number of difficulties which may be encountered when interacting with non-handicapped children.

The opportunity for such a programme may well be provided by a special class or unit, where security is offered, but where contact with the non-handicapped is also possible. Physically handicapped children have fewer initial social encounters than their non-handicapped peers, and lack of mobility reduces opportunities for initiating social relationships. Feelings of discouragement and unwantedness may be born out of experiences of rebuffing. The non-handicapped child likely to initiate contact with the handicapped child is generally more isolated than normal, has less general social experience and may not have acquired accurate peer group values.

Such a child may feel the physically handicapped child is less threatening and competitive and is therefore more likely to accept him. The child who likes others to be dependent upon him will also be attracted to a child who is handicapped. Thus the handicapped child is supplying a need for the insecure non-handicapped child.

Clearly there are dangers in 'stage managing' friendships, but this should not prevent the establishment of conditions that encourage constructive interactions and foster the growth of friendships. The classroom teacher possesses day-to-day knowledge of the degree of interaction amongst pupils in the class and can influence that interaction in a direct ongoing way. How the teacher creates the classroom environment and structures the activities within it is the single most important factor in promoting integration.

School attainment

Warnock said: 'The purpose of education for all children is the same; the goals are the same. But, the help that individual children need in progressing towards them will be different.' Hegarty and Pocklington (1981) suggest that the curriculum available to pupils and the specific programmes of work selected from it, must match their special needs, as well as take account of the educational environment in which they find themselves. The classroom teacher is the key to creating this environment.

There is considerable diversity in practice of the curriculum on offer to pupils with special needs in mainstream schools. The possible effects of learning disabilities mean that many physically handicapped children and young people may make only limited progress towards the goals of individual development, which enables them to become active responsible members of society. However, if the curriculum comprises formal activities devised by the school to achieve objectives, and hence meet the special needs, then it follows that the school's curriculum will reflect the nature of its pupils and the levels of ability by which they achieve. Changes will be affected by the opportunities the mainstream school presents and the constraints it imposes.

An *objectives* approach to curriculum planning concentrates on those classroom factors which can be controlled by the teacher in the classroom situation, and rests on defining teaching goals, breaking them down into precisely stated and carefully sequenced objectives, and monitoring pupils' progress through continuous and systematic assessment. This might well be the context within which curriculum options are selected or developed, in integration programmes for physically handicapped pupils with associated learning disabilities. Such an approach might be considered a major step forward in minimizing the possible effects of learning disabilities on academic achievement and attainment.

It is stressed, however, that a normal curriculum necessitates some modification for pupils with specific learning disabilities, to ensure attainment is achieved in appropriate skills. Chapter 7 outlines a practical approach to this task, and gives an insight into essential components. A prime consideration must be the provision of a structured teaching programme, designed to ensure mastery of the basics of numeracy and literacy, and the acquiring of essential social skills. In addition, 'continuous curricular assessment and development, along with individual educational programmes and individual timetables, are the means of producing a challenging, enriching, and educationally sound curriculum' (Brennan, 1982a).

Failure to learn, whether in terms of cognitive skills and other aspects of formal education; in the broad field of relationships; or in general social development, is intensely personal and idiosyncratic, as is success. One of the most striking facts is that almost any combination of adverse factors may be associated with failure, or be found in success. The only fully established difference is that children who are failing have, on average, more adverse factors than successful children. Many such factors are associated with handicap.

Wall (1979) suggests that if a threshold of difficulty is low or resources high, then the balance will move to success. If the threshold of difficulty is high or the resources low, then failure will result. It must be acknowledged however, that a high proportion of children with considerable special educational needs, and adverse factors in their environment, do make sound academic achievements and reach a high level of attainment.

An accurate assessment of the child's learning difficulties, of his assets and liabilities, and the development of a realistic programme of education, will combat the possible effects of learning disabilities on educational achievement. Such assessment and planning must be concerned with the whole development of the child and, ideally, would actively involve all those dealing with the handicapped child.

Some of the problems which affect the learning processes arise from defects in the central nervous system, defects in hearing and sight, and speech difficulties. Defects in hearing and sight can have severe consequences for speech development, for general cognitive growth, and for development from percept to concept. Neurological damage or disturbance can affect the ability to grasp early comprehension skills or achieve motor co-ordination and this will affect a young child's exploration of objects and of himself. Lack of or uncertainty in cerebral dominance, will make life more difficult and less rewarding, and when a child is making attempts at formal learning, such imperfections may interpose hindrances both in social integration and in establishing the left-to-right sequence, an important aspect of deciphering the printed page of writing. A further important area is that of speech, and speech difficulties may be one of a number of symptoms of neurological disturbance or damage. A deficiency, defect or derangement of speech is a serious impediment to general learning and socialization. Poor speech can also interfere with, or be a reflection of, other aspects of development which may well affect achievement and attainment, in educational terms.

The following chapters will establish that the ideal system for the education of handicapped children is neither full integration nor complete segregation. Rather, the book will show there should be an integrated and co-ordinated special educational system, allowing placement of children to be dependent upon the needs of the individual child, and the capacity of the school to meet them. Medical diagnosis alone is not a sufficiently strong basis for deciding educational placement.

The concept of handicap is a broad and complex one, and it is not easy to define handicapping conditions in terms which convey the same meaning to everyone, or even to decide precisely what constitutes a handicap, at a particular age. This book is essentially concerned with the functional aspects of handicap, that is, what effect the handicap has on the child's daily performance. Chapter 2 outlines the design of the study, and the methodology chosen to elicit information from three main areas which directly influenced the results of the investigation. A wide knowledge of each area leads to the correlation of relevant information which establishes an appraisal of the factors which contribute to programmes of successful integration.

Part II

Design of the Study

2
Description and Methodology

The background to the study shows, initially, to what degree the attitudes of those professional agencies involved with assisting parents in selecting the type of education as the most appropriate to meet the child's special educational needs, influence their decisions. The problems are discussed with reference to different groups involved; administrators; teachers both *special* and *mainstream*; handicapped children and their families; the non-handicapped peers and their parents. In the following chapters the points are outlined in greater detail and the fieldwork discussed.

Comparisons between the Sample Group and Control Groups were made in terms of educational attainment, socialization and emotional development using standardized and non-standardized testing materials for children of primary school age. An evaluation of the nature and purpose of interaction between non-handicapped and handicapped pupils in integrated situations was made through regular visits to schools to meet, informally, both handicapped and non-handicapped pupils. Observations were made of numerous integrated activities; educational, social and recreational, and resultant problems were determined, difficulties discussed, and appropriate advice given for resolution. Educational ability and social aptitude was assessed through oral and written questionnaires, and patterns of educational attainment and social adjustment were monitored and analysed in both the Sample and Control Groups. Specific consideration was given to establish how the nature of the organization of any particular type of provision influenced the success of, and enhanced the purpose of, integration.

It was, essentially, the intention of the research to identify what prerequisites were necessary to meet the special needs of the physically handicapped child, to enable both handicapped and non-handicapped pupils to fully benefit from integrated education. The conditions which help to reduce the problems and so promote successful integration are discussed and consideration was specifically given to the determination of demands placed upon schools who are integrating severely disabled children into mainstream classes. The extent by which the major functional effect of the physical handicap influences, realistically, parental expectations, was examined, to determine whether the presence of disorders affecting the central nervous system were a prime cause of educational problems in mainstream schools. Finally, how the severity of a child's physical handicap might relate to his educational progress in the mainstream classroom situation, to his social adjustment in it, or to his popularity amongst his non-handicapped peers, was identified. The study concluded with an analysis of these factors, and the degree to which the integration of physically handicapped pupils was successful.

The study, albeit small scale, sought to describe and analyse the organization and structure of three distinct forms of integrated provision for physically handicapped children, along various dimensions relevant to practice, using interview and observational material as well as quantitative data. However, because the study was small scale, the findings should not be seen as representative of all schemes of integrated provision for pupils with special educational needs, within LEAs.

The schools

Initially, a written approach was made to LEAs in the London boroughs and surrounding Home Counties, for information as to how many physically handicapped children were attending mainstream primary schools, either on an individual or group basis. The nature of the study required that schools be specifically selected, and it was necessary from a personal point of view for the areas where the schools were situated to be within reasonable travelling distance from the London area.

In selecting the survey schools, a comparison in location was deliberately sought. The local environment and community were considered, and the schools' relationship with the same were examined. The schools in one Home County were all situated in industrial areas, highly populated, and with relevant problems of unemployment and low socio-economic status. By contrast, the schools in the second Home County were rurally situated, but adjacent to small towns with an above average level of employment, average populations, and high socio-economic status. The schools in two London boroughs were located in highly contrasting areas, yet both had the common factor of a large immigrant population, and in parts were industrial, with a full range of socio-economic levels. Areas of information sought concerned the size of the schools; internal organization and class grouping; use of staffing resources, in respect of handicapped pupils; the curriculum and the criteria which influenced its planning. The need for and the establishment of the programme of integration is examined, and its subsequent development discussed. Table 2.1 indicates the criteria for admission to the integration programmes in the nine survey schools, and suggests how the criteria influences the type of programme which the individual schools offer.

In my view, it was important to include the more severely physically handicapped pupils in the Sample Group, in order to highlight the areas of difficulty experienced by the schools examined, in making special educational provision, and to identify the essential prerequisites necessary to meet the special needs of the pupils. It would seem that the promotion of a reasonable level of independence and functional ability might be relative to academic achievement and attainment. A number of schools were visited therefore, before the final selection was made.

The study is concerned with three distinct types of integration. Schools *A*, *D* and *G* adopted the format of a normal class with care support for the pupil with special needs. This type of integrated provision is distinctively characteristic, given that resources are dispersed and brought to the pupil rather than being concentrated in one area. The integrated provision organized in Schools *C*, *E* and *F* took the form of a normal class, with support for the teacher and pupil within the class, and facilities for withdrawal for specialist work. This provision operates to a resource model and allows for two main possibilities – withdrawal to a resource facility which is a permanent part of the school; and

Table 2.1   Type of integration programme and criteria for admission

Type of Programme	Schools	Criteria for admission to full-time integration programme
1. Non-selective programme of integration	School C	The ability to integrate into and contribute to all aspects of school life.
	School E	Any pupil whose major handicap is physical, with the understanding of the LEA and parents, that if placement, after a reasonable period of time, proves to be over-problematic or unsuccessful, the pupil will be transferred to a more suitable educational environment.
	School F	Any physically handicapped pupil who the school believes will respond to an appropriate education relevant to his/her needs, in either the special resource class or the normal classroom situation. The child must have a reasonable degree of independence and be able to make reasonable progress. Any physically handicapped pupil on a trial basis.
2. Campus integration programme	School B	Physically handicapped pupils must be able to walk, albeit with walking aids or frame. Class areas too small for wheelchairs.
	School H	An average level of ability, and whether or not the school feels it can help the child. Handicapped pupils are not treated differently, and hence must have a positive attitude towards independence.
	School I	The child must be capable of receiving a normal education, and must have a satisfactory medical prognosis.
3. Selective programme of integration	School A	No specific criteria. Consideration for placement would be given, at the request of parents, LEA or the headteacher of local special school.
	School D	Ability of the school to cope with physical management of the handicap; suitable access and to provide for the special educational needs.
	School G	No specific criteria. If there is a suitable vacancy, and if, in the school's opinion, the physically handicapped child is of average intelligence. Could not accommodate pupils with both severe physical handicaps and learning difficulties.

withdrawal for specialist help provided on a peripatetic basis. A popular form of integration was found in schools *B*, *H* and *I*, where the normal class was used as a base, with withdrawal for specialist work to a special resource centre, or where the special resource centre served as the base, with participation in activities in the normal class on a part-time basis.

The factors which influenced the final selection of schools, and hence the Sample Group, were:

(a) the severity of physical handicap amongst pupils participating in the integration programme;
(b) the presence of an associated learning disability amongst the majority of the handicapped children who were integrated;
(c) the location of the schools, providing a socio-economic and cultural basis for comparison, in parental expectation and pupil achievement.

The Sample Group

The final group of 50 children selected for the survey were all classified as severely physically handicapped; some with associated learning difficulties and others from multicultural backgrounds. The Sample Group, ranging in age from 4.4 years to 12.6 years, were selected from the schools where the headteachers and their staffs saw the active involvement in the Research Project as a purposeful resource for further developing their existing systems of integrated education. This enthusiastic commitment and desire to assimilate new and further knowledge in a creative and purposeful way, is a positive step towards successful integration.

The 50 children came from each of the three groups of schools, and in each group, schools were selected where integration was organized on a group basis, and where provision was individually arranged. All the physically handicapped children attending the particular schools are included in the Sample Group, and the following data gives an indication of the number and percentage of physically handicapped pupils in the group in four distinct categories:

(a) pupils with neurological disorders – 17 : 34 per cent of Sample Group;

(b) pupils with associated learning difficulties – 15 : 30 per cent of Sample Group;
(c) pupils with secondary handicaps – 12 : 24 per cent of Sample Group;
(d) pupils from multicultural backgrounds – 10 : 20 per cent of Sample Group.

As can be seen from the design of the study, specific consideration was given to the relevance of the presence in one or more of the above categories, of those pupils in the Sample Group, and the implications of these factors for integration are discussed later. Table 2.2 gives the handicaps of the pupils in the Sample Group.

Table 2.2   Sample Group: handicaps

Handicap	Number	Percentage	
Spina Bifida	3	6%	⎫ 24%
Spina Bifida with Hydrocephalus	9	18%	⎭
Cerebral Palsy	10	20%	
Brain Damage	5	10%	
Muscular Atrophy	5	10%	
Muscular Dystrophy	3	6%	
Arthrogryposis	2	4%	
Haemophilia	2	4%	
Imperforate Anus	2	4%	
Rheumatoid Arthritis	2	4%	
Congenital Heart Disease	1	2%	
Familial Rickets	1	2%	
Lower Limb Paralysis	1	2%	
Osteogenesis Imperfecta (Brittle Bones)	1	2%	
Poliomyelitis	1	2%	
Rubella Syndrome	1	2%	
Siamese Twin	1	2%	
Total	50	100%	

The Sample Group was divided into two further groups:

(a) a large group of 31 *middle school* pupils, aged from 7.7 years to 12.6 years attending mainstream junior, middle or primary schools; and
(b) 19 *first school* pupils aged 4.4 years to 9 years attending mainstream infants/first schools or classes (Appendix A).

In the junior/middle school group, all those pupils attending the schools and classified as severely physically handicapped were included. Mildly and moderately handicapped pupils were excluded as ordinary school placement poses few problems for them. In the infant/first school group, the aim of the method of selection was to obtain a small group of handicapped children placed in a mainstream or special class, and for whom some sort of 'special' provision was required. The findings, which illustrate how these pupils are functioning and the adequacy of the provision made for them, will give some idea of the feasibility of placing severely handicapped children in mainstream schools, and an indication of the major problems involved and related. Hence, children with handicaps whose effects were likely to pose serious problems in a mainstream school owing, for example, to incontinence, severely restricted mobility, severe haemophilia, or specific learning disabilities, were selected. This small group was, thus, a highly selective sample.

The Control Group

The Control Group consisted of 100 children, i.e. two pupils were nominated by class teachers to represent each handicapped pupil, thus forming two Control Groups. The teachers were asked to nominate non-handicapped pupils of above average and below average ability, basing their selection on personal assessment in terms of all-round classroom performance. The findings in respect of the levels of attainment and achievement by the two groups might have been significantly different, however, had nominations been based on standardized test results. One of the intentions of the practical investigation was to note the position of the physically handicapped child within the class group, in terms of social and emotional adaptation, and academic achievement and attainment. Had time allowed, it is possible that the position of the handicapped child within the class group would have been different if the numbers of non-handicapped pupils in the Control Groups had been greater. The Control Groups were therefore used to illustrate the position of the Sample Group of physically handicapped children, using the two extremes.

Wherever possible ages were matched, but this factor was not dominant in the nomination of the Control Groups.

Data collection

To obtain information about the integrated provision for severely physically handicapped pupils in the four LEAs, headteachers, teachers-in-charge, and teachers directly involved with the integration programmes in the nine survey schools were interviewed. The interview (Appendix B) sought information on:

  – the general admissions policy of the school;
  – practices and policies relating to accepting handicapped pupils;
  – views on the integration of handicapped pupils of primary age within mainstream schools;
  – relationships with parents and professional agencies, in respect of matters concerned directly with handicap;
  – the assessment and treatment of handicap;
  – facilities for the handicapped;
  – the future provision planned for handicapped pupils with associated learning difficulties.

Class teachers were asked to complete a questionnaire which asked for basic data about:

  – ability expectation;
  – learning problems associated with handicap;
  – social interaction with non-handicapped peers;
  – their views on the integration of the handicapped child in the mainstream classroom environment (Appendix C).

Personal interviews were also held with teachers, ancillary and therapy staffs, LEA personnel, educational psychologists and specialists in child health, involved with the recommendation for integrated education. These were designed to identify the problems and needs of the handicapped pupil and to establish in which areas of development and behaviour specialist help is being, or could be, of benefit. Particular note was taken of the amount of information and advice received by the teacher and the school about the pupil and his special needs. Other information was sought about:

- the child's dependence upon aids for mobility and educational activities;
- the resultant quality of attainment and interaction;
- his social adaptation and adjustment skills;
- his behaviour in the class or group;
- his position in the family, and the extent of parental contact and involvement with the school.

Assessment of the Sample Group

Assessment of the Sample Group was based on parents' and teachers' observations, and on the pupils' personal achievements in terms of educational attainment, socialization and emotional development. Brief descriptions of the instruments used for assessing the children are given below.

(a)   Teachers: personal interview   (1)

The aim was to provide a comprehensive picture of the children's functioning and behaviour, as seen through the eyes of teachers who had been in regular contact with the pupils for several months. Teachers were asked to describe the educational response of the school to the observations which they made. It was intended that discussion would contribute to the development of assessment techniques, which are based on teachers' observations, and would help to link these to a planned educational response. Areas for which contributions were sought included:

1. The making of judgements as to whether the functioning or behaviour of the pupil with special needs was outside the 'normal range' and, if so, whether any special action had been taken, or was planned.
2. The identification of any specific educational activities in the classroom environment which had proved especially beneficial in tackling pupils' special needs.

3. How far the pupils' special needs were being met, the extent of specialist provision required, the severity of the handicap and associated difficulties, particularly in relation to learning, and the effect of the handicap on the child's participation in classroom activities, and any subsequent restrictions.

Questionnaire   (2)

As well as seeking factual information on matters such as the child's placement in the class, the professional advice which the teacher had received, and the teacher's contact with parents, the questionnaire gave teachers the opportunity for descriptive comment on the handicapped child's achievements, on his behaviour and adjustment within the class, and on any problems which his presence posed for the class group (Appendix C).

(b)   Parents: personal interview and questionnaire

Although the information gleaned was mainly concerned with family background, and the meeting of the child's special needs within the home environment, parents were asked to make an assessment of the handicapped child's behaviour, social adjustment, and educational achievement. Attitudes of the parents towards the integration programme were ascertained, and its suitability for the individual child with special needs assessed in the light of the views expressed. Additionally, the information assimilated through the parents' questionnaire classified the family according to parental occupation, socio-economic standard of living, and family size and stability (Appendix D).

To ascertain the attitudes and expectations of the parents towards integration, further home interviews were arranged with 25, approximately 50 per cent of the families of the Sample Group.

The interview took the form of the parents' questionnaire initially, which led to more detailed information being given and views expressed about basic family data; adaptations to the home; the nature of advice, guidance and support received by the parents; the role of other members of the family and friends in meeting the needs of the handicapped child; home-based help and aids provided, and the education and future placement of the child. In spite of the comprehensive and personal nature of the interview, the parents were most co-operative and gave generously of their time. Additionally, parents of the pupils in the Sample Group were met at informal school functions and hence meetings with one or both parents of a further 20 handicapped pupils were achieved.

The reaction of the parents of pupils in the Control Groups to the presence of physically handicapped pupils in their children's classes was of particular interest and is discussed in Chapter 3. Information about the home and family was ascertained from the pupils themselves, and from a number of parents of pupils in the Control Group, who were met also at school functions and organized 'in-school' activities.

The techniques of personal interview coupled with questionnaire were likely to provide a more objective assessment of the facilities, amenities and other educational provisions of a school or special class, but gave no indication of the quality of education which the school provided. The data sought for the practical investigation focused on items relating to the education of primary age physically handicapped children, and the physical attributes of the school building, its location and internal adaptations and facilities, in respect of meeting the special needs of its pupils.

(c) The pupils

All the children in the Sample Group and Control Groups in the appropriate test age range were individually assessed. The following standardized tests were used:

1. Neale Analysis of Reading Ability: Test B

The objective scores for fluency, accuracy and comprehension, which this test provides, compare the performance of the physically handicapped pupil with the average performance of children of the same age. The individual Record Sheet designed for use with the test facilitates the noting of *types* of errors and characteristics, and provides a test summary of objective scores and a number of characteristics concerning an individual's approach to oral reading, his speech, mannerisms, word recognition skills, etc. Such characteristics are critical in assessing the performance of the physically handicapped child, given that the handicapping condition may directly affect such characteristics.

2. National Foundation for Educational Research: Basic
   Mathematics Tests: Tests A – DE

The tests aim to give some diagnostic information about a child's individual strengths and weaknesses. Such information can be valuable to the teacher in directing children's mathematical learning and can, in particular, establish a pattern of learning difficulties in respect of mathematical concepts in specific handicapping conditions.

The following non-standardized test was used:

3. Barker Lunn Primary Children's Attitude Scales

The 10 attitude scales, for use with 9 – 11-year-old children, are intended for research purposes to examine broad group differences. The ten scales are:

A. Attitude to school
B. Interest in school work
C. Importance of doing well at school
D. Attitude to class
E. 'Other' image of class
F. Conforming versus non-conforming pupil
G. Relationship with teacher
H. Anxiety in the classroom situation
I. Social adjustment – getting on well with classmates
J. Academic self-image.

Group discussions with the classes generally were held, with the aim of determining what attitudes the children held and how these feelings were expressed. Thus the objective of this exploratory work was to obtain a representative picture of the way children view school.

4. Effectiveness motivation

During the investigation continuous contact was made with the children, on average at intervals of two weeks over one academic year, in class and school activity situations, and observation of adult – child interaction established the nature of stimulation received.

The concept of 'effectiveness motivation' is especially relevant to the problems of severely physically handicapped children, integrated in mainstream primary schools. This concept is described by Sharp and Stott (1976), in Chazan *et al* (1980), 'in terms of the ways in which the child finds the outcomes of curiosity, discovery, recognition, production of an effect of change, and exercise of control over his environment reinforcing, and productive of, further effort'. The other assessment instruments aimed to find out what the child could or could not do, and to estimate levels of competence in specific areas of function. So, in contrast, observation based on 'effectiveness motivation' assesses the general level of those activities which enable a child to demonstrate to himself, or others, increased effectiveness in controlling or influencing his own environment.

Part III

The Practical Investigation

3
Parents in Integration

To the principle of integration, parents and professionals bring differing perspectives. These perspectives can be a source of strength in developing educational programmes for pupils with special needs, or a source of conflict which may result in misinterpretation in communication, if each party fails to understand the other's perspective. McCall (1983) observed that in the complex area of human development it is rare that either party can be totally 'right' or 'wrong', and he believes that what is essentially required is a realistic attempt by both to define their expectations, and a desire to work towards the fulfilment of such expectation, matching what is taught to needs.

From a professional point of view, group learning of all kinds is a facet of *out-of-school* activity, as much as within. The parent, like the teacher, can create very varied social experiences for their children, which allow opportunity for observation in a variety of contexts. They arc often able to identify the group needs of their child, and advise as to the child's reactions to and benefits from, the different kinds of school-based and classroom-based group activities. Brennan (1982a) suggests that whilst the selection, organization and presentation of the specific learning experiences, through which pupils are to attain their curricular objectives, are the concern of the classroom teacher, parents and others have a legitimate and valuable contribution in selecting guiding aims and helping modification of such aims as a result of feedback from curricular activities. Hence the recognition of the critical importance of the school's partnership with parents; successful learning depends on the right kind of parent – school relationships.

Parents can only fulfil this role in integration adequately if teachers explain in detail their curricular intentions, and involve parents in the purposes of classroom group experience. Essentially, parents require clear information and sensitive support. Many welcome involvement of their expertise and the onus is clearly on teachers to recognize parents' rights regarding the assessment of and placement of their child (Education Act 1981). Equally, teachers require accurate sources of information regarding parents' needs, rights, and talents, to use such knowledge to promote opportunities for explaining group learning and assessment approaches, and to seek ways of involving parents in some activities, where and whenever possible. Integration is, in a sense, a new situation for many parents, and presents different opportunities for home and school contact and collaboration, whilst entailing new roles as well. The role of parents in integration is influenced, primarily, by four interrelated factors: their attitudes towards integration; the amount and nature of their contact with the school; the function of home and school contact; and the promotion of parental involvement.

Attitudes towards integration

An undisputed finding which emerged from the practical investigation was that parents wanted integration for their children with special educational needs. The 40 parents with whom direct contact was made all wanted their children to continue their education in an integrated environment, although seven acknowledged that because of their child's gross disabilities, education in a specialist facility might well be necessary at a later stage. One parent of a severely handicapped non-communicative cerebral palsied child said: 'I shall always be so very grateful that he was given the chance to attend a normal school. I know he will have to go away to a residential special school as he gets older, but at least he wasn't just written off.' Parents' attitudes towards integration can be considered as a desire for normality; concern for academic progress, and experience of, and attitudes towards, special schools. The most recurrent theme related to normality – after experiencing the pain and frustration of having their child singled out as different, they wanted him to be given the opportunity to be as normal as possible. Parents were not unaware of the need for special help and to some extent were dependent on this. Their desire for normality was not a rejecting of this help, but they did reject forms of help they saw as inappropriate. Clearly, they wanted help in a context of normality, and saw placement in a mainstream school as such. Although several parents appreciated their children were different from their non-handicapped peers in major ways, and their expectations for their children from mainstream school placement were limited, they undoubtedly felt the placement had achieved a very great deal. Parents described normality as an end in itself; the promotion of maturity and personal development; growth in independence; implications for how handicap is viewed; and benefits to the parents themselves.

All the parents interviewed were anxious that their handicapped child should get as good an education as possible. The majority, some 75 per cent, stated they were very satisfied with their child's progress at school, and their expectations of integration had been admirably met. Table 3.1 gives their responses in this respect.

Table 3.1 Parental satisfaction with progress

Dissatisfied	Reasonably satisfied	Very satisfied
0	7	36

The parents strongly endorsed the school's efforts, and in response to the question about their child's level of ability, in the main they were realistic and reasonably accurate in their estimate as to how well their child was getting on with his/her school work.

Table 3.2 Parental estimate of progress

Don't know	Making slow progress	Little below ave.	About ave.	Above ave.
0	6	9	21	7

The questionnaire for parents asked if they felt on the whole that the school was the right kind for their child. The following responses represent the views:

'We are thrilled with his progress since he went to this marvellous school.'

'Since going to school, he has made excellent all round development and achieved things we never thought possible.'

'The school has met her needs so very well. We are absolutely delighted.'

'She is so happy there, and has taken on a new lease of life since she went to the school. She is now keenly interested in everything, and wants to work.'

'I am disappointed that he may now have to attend a special school. I feel if the school had a nurse, my son's physical handicap would not present such a problem. It seems that he is unable to learn to do things because he is so handicapped.'

'Although we feel the school is the right place for her, we are a little disappointed with her lack of academic progress. We feel that a teacher qualified and experienced to teach children with learning difficulties is what the school needs, to help our daughter and others like her.'

This enthusiastic endorsement of the academic provision within integration programmes is in sharp contrast to the parents' perceptions of the schooling their children had received in special schools. Of the 18 pupils in the sample group who had transferred from special schools, only eight parents felt their children had received an education on a par with that of a mainstream school, and this was attributed to the headteacher of the special school where all eight children attended, who considered education the main priority and provided the same curriculum for her pupils as in every other borough primary school. The general impression given by the other ten parents was that their children's special schools offered little more than a childminding service, and that their children were grouped with severely retarded pupils, and hence were contained in an abysmal environment, totally devoid of stimulus. They suggested their children were not being stretched, that they were offered a very narrow, watered-down curriculum, and hence were certainly not making measurable progress of any kind. Typical comments were:

'There was not much education at the special school – run by ladies in white coats and aprons, who are too preoccupied with the

physical handicaps – education is "fit in" if there is time.'
'Going to a mainstream school has been good for Andrew – it has
made him work – he was left to do as he liked in the special school,
in a class of near idiots.'
'Educational standards at the special school were appalling – she
wasn't getting any education comparable with her ability. Nobody
knows the worry which this caused my husband and I.'

The sample group of parents involved in the practical investigation tended, on the whole, to regard special schools as artificial,
sheltered environments, as 'institutional' and as lacking in stimulation. Their reactions are perhaps not surprising, given that many
of the parents had chosen or agreed willingly to integration, and
some had fought hard to keep their child out of special schooling.
At the same time, they were aware of a number of advantages of
special schools. They acknowledged the availability of
individualized and specialized attention, from suitably trained and
experienced teachers, who understood the child's difficulties and
problems, that special schools might be in a better position to
resolve the problems, and to promote independence by means of
specific training in areas of mobility and social skills, but, as one
parent firmly stated, 'at the expense of an education involving the
broader aspects of the curriculum'. However, all in all, parents
seemed genuinely convinced that their children were getting the
right kind of education and that the advantages of integration
outweighed the disadvantages.

Only a very small number of parents expressed some disappointment with the progress their child with special educational needs
was making in the mainstream school, but in general terms they
were reasonably satisfied, in view of their children's limitations,
and keenly supported integration in principle. It is, however, of
relevance to comment here that three of these children are being
transferred to special schools, and a further two are awaiting
assessment for residential special school placements. This small
group of five parents agreed without hesitation that their children
had clearly benefited socially by placement in a mainstream school,
and had all been extremely happy and made a great many friends.
In a further two cases a source of dissatisfaction centred around
disagreement over the school's assessment of the child's capacities
and abilities. The number of parents involved here is small, but

their views give further support to the general preference for mainstream school placement.

Family and home needs

We need to consider how the family as a whole perceive their needs, and what kinds of demands are made on other members of the family by the needs of the child in integrated education, and the expertise of professionals involved in this provision. Emotional reactions and practical realities determine the nature and degree of any possible partnerships. At pre-school level, the main link will be the professional services working with handicapped children and their families in their homes, and contributing to assessment at that level. An important part of their task will be contact with, and advice about, playgroups, nursery schools, toy libraries and other sources of educational support for the children and their families. In two LEAs, an advisory and support service were actively involved in pre-school provision. Such a service sought to reassure parents about school placement, the routines associated with placement, the outcome of reviews concerning their child, and to assist with any educational problem causing concern. Disagreements between parents and professional agencies will require that a special education adviser is afforded the right to advise parents exclusively on the basis of what is the best special educational provision to meet the child's special needs. Twelve parents stated they had had no support from professional agencies, other than their child's school, and hence could have no confidence in 'alleged' support services.

Parents expressed dissatisfaction with the arrangements for school medical examinations in seven out of the nine survey schools. Generally, they felt it inopportune that the headteacher and the classroom teacher were not invited to be present at medical examinations. One parent felt it was difficult for her to appreciate how the work of the district health authority specialists could relate to the teacher and educational activities, when education personnel were unable to participate in relevant discussion. Another mother felt that the presence of several women when the examination was taking place was of great embarrassment to her son, and she further felt this was an erosion of privacy and

dignity. Only nine parents agreed that school medical examinations were useful in that they provided opportunity for medical
officers, therapists, health visitors and social workers to discuss
their child with them, and explain their work in respect of the
individual child with special needs. More than 75 per cent of the
parents felt the examinations were a waste of time, given that
nearly every physically handicapped child attended a hospital
regularly.

It was noted, amongst the sample group of handicapped
children studied, that in the instances of integration held to be
most successful, teachers remarked on the high degree of home
support. This is perhaps not surprising, given that the majority of
parents firmly supported the concept of integration, and hence it is
reasonable to assume that they will actively assist their child to
make progress. Another relevant factor was the number of
references made by members of the educational and medical
professions as to the need for greater recognition of the value of
the *good* home environment – further evidence of an increasing
awareness that parents should be helped to play a fuller role in
their child's education. However, as one headteacher aptly pointed out, it is possible that home and school place greater emphasis
upon different ends. The school, she pointed out, lacking the
emotional attachment that parents have, may emphasize
academic ends. Parents, by contrast, may see little beyond the
immediate future, desiring only that their child experiences a
normal and decent education. Many parents are content that their
child is happy at school, and, indeed, the happiness of the child
with special needs is of paramount importance in relation to
security, in both the school and home environment.

It is of interest to consider how mothers see their handicapped
child, in terms of temperament and of being easy to manage. Such
assessment would appear to bear specific relation to parental
expectation of the success of mainstream school placement. One
question in the questionnaire for families asked whether the
handicapped child is *'usually happy or is he/she quite often
miserable?'* The majority of parents, some 84 per cent, thought of
their children as being happy most of the time – this does not mean
that the children are never miserable at all but that families are
prepared, it might be assumed, to tolerate justifiable upsets,
particularly when they realize their children are, understandably,

bored with the limited range of activities and amusements open to them. They still, in the main, think of their children as being quite happy, after making these allowances. In response to the question as to whether their child has ever said that everything seems hopeless and that nothing is worthwhile, only three mothers, six per cent of the total, had experienced this, always when the child was preparing for major surgery, had suffered greatly from surgery, or had spent long periods of time in hospital. The question '*Is there a problem of misery or depression?*' brought the response that some children are very quiet and appear apathetic, but there are always good reasons for them feeling miserable, indicated ten mothers, who felt their children are as happy as they can be, given the circumstances. The majority of the children were considered to be relatively easy to manage by their families, but eight children, 16 per cent in total, were not. They were said to be awkward to handle in a physical sense, in that they simply wanted to do things for themselves and be independent, and hence resented needing help. In five cases, where gross handicap meant total dependence, certain activities were extremely time-consuming, and resulted in somewhat fraught situations.

The parents of these grossly handicapped children clearly recognized the severe restraints imposed on the class teacher and the school in general by their child's presence. They all accepted without any hesitation that their child would eventually require placement in a special school or a specialist facility, because of the severe limitations of their handicaps. This healthy acceptance, realistically, might be attributed to successful school and parent partnerships, where the two parties have worked together towards agreed aims and goals, resulting in purposeful integration within the limits of severe handicapping conditions. There was no evidence of resentment, failure, or lack of understanding, but a good deal of evidence of positive liaison and planning which had allowed these pupils with special needs, attending schools *E* and *F*, to have achieved maximum educational, social and emotional benefit, from integrated provision. In one parent's words:

> he can now accept his handicap, and what it means, because he has come to realize at his normal school that the non-handicapped like him and will help him just as much as they do each other. Being amongst non-handicapped children has helped him

to realize there are some things he can do, and some things he cannot, just like all children, and this has helped him to overcome his feelings of being a failure. He no longer feels threatened by whatever lies ahead.

Clearly evident was the trust and confidence of parents and all survey schools, in each other, and there were only two instances of parents blaming the school for their child's failure educationally. In both cases, the children had severe learning difficulties, and partnership between school and parent was nonexistent.

The sample group of parents agreed unanimously that it was invaluable for their child to grow up in a normal environment. Several parents mentioned the encouragement which it gave them to see casual friendships developing between their child and other school children, which they felt signified the acceptance of their child as just another child, and not as handicapped. Fourteen parents referred to an escalation in personal development and maturity when their child was placed in a mainstream school. One parent commented that on transfer from special to mainstream school, within a term she noticed her child developing a more outgoing personality and a greater spirit of independence. Another parent stated: 'By the end of his first term at school, we could just not believe he was the same child. His self-esteem had grown in "leaps and bounds" and he was much more livelier.' These are typical of many comments from parents who observed that their child had come out of his shell, related to people better, and had generally grown up, as a result of mixing with normal children. A growth in a feeling of security for the handicapped child was reflected in parents' attitudes to teasing. They were not only unconcerned about it, generally, but occasionally observed that this was something their children would have to learn to cope with anyway. One parent said: 'This is a part of learning to live with their handicapping conditions', and another felt that 'taking the rough with the smooth is teaching them to respond naturally and "matter of factly" to such situations.' A further aspect of maturing, particularly valued by parents, was the greater independence that they felt integration promoted – 'she stands up for herself more now'.

Parents were anxious for their children to have the experience of mixing with non-handicapped children and people – segregation was not healthy. Integration was of benefit to other non-handicapped children, in that they were helped to gain an understanding and appreciate the problems of handicap. Eighty per cent of the parents voiced this feeling, in respect to other children in their families – through having everyday contact with handicap, they had the opportunity to become accustomed to handicap, and develop realistic attitudes towards it. Besides benefiting those with special needs, regular contact assists in eradicating negative and hostile images of the handicapped child, and provides a valuable learning experience for other pupils. This, the parents felt, was of great importance.

A number of parents, nine in total, indicated the immense relief they felt when their child was accepted for placement in a mainstream school. As one parent described: 'the first few years were full of disappointment, feelings of guilt and failure, but after being accepted at a normal school, hope began, and we found it easier to accept him as our child.' Such acceptance was remarked upon by several parents who felt it had become easier to accept their handicapped child, once his school days began in the mainstream school, like everyone else's child. Parents can run the risk of seeing their handicapped children first as handicapped and secondly as children, so it is worthy of note that a small number of them, seven, acknowledged that having their child attend a mainstream school helped them reverse that order. There were instances where active parental pressure for a place at a particular school, or for a particular type of education, had clearly been influential. The parents of ten children in the sample group were determined to resist pressure for special schooling, and their assertiveness was rewarded. In four cases, where the headteachers of the local mainstream schools had agreed to accept physically handicapped children as pupils, the result had been the initiation and development of two integration programmes. It is significant to remark here, however, that these four pupils are rated as being amongst the most intellectually able pupils at their schools.

Ideally, parents should be clearly informed of the reasons for recommended placements, and their agreement and co-operation sought. Research has shown that the psychosocial, rather than the physical factor, is the major determinant in the placement decision, and has acknowledged there to be wide differences and enormous variations between local education authorities, with regard to the amount, and type, of special provision available in mainstream schools. Certainly, general trends are becoming clearer, but it is arguable, given the Education Act 1981, that parents have been afforded any substantial rights to choose where their handicapped child might be educated. It is still the case that for many parents of handicapped children, the possibility of suitable provision being made depends very much on chance, that is, on where they happen to live. The findings of this Survey indicated that where special school placement had been suggested by the various professional agencies, the strength with which the recommendation had been made matched the persistence which the parents had to display in order to obtain mainstream school placement. This aspect will be discussed fully in Chapter 5. However, there has over the past decade been growing participation by parents in policy formation at local, national and international levels. Parents are increasingly participating in decision-making, affecting the planning, development and operation of educational services. At local level, for example, more parent representatives are now acting as school governors, as members of community health councils and as members of joint care planning teams which were established from 1976 onwards, to work for greater effective collaboration between health and local authority services. The movement for participation is still growing, however, and in only two of the nine survey schools, was a parent of a handicapped child a member of the school governing body. One other parent had recently been invited to join the local community health council.

Home–school liaison

A number of earlier studies contrasting the relative influence of home and school on children's intellectual and educational achievements, support the view that the influence of the home is comparatively greater in the early years, and that children who come from homes where the parents take an active interest in their child's education, tend to have higher school attainments – this influence is even greater where handicapped children are concerned. Growth and learning in children can only be understood in relation to the various environments in which the child is living.

The importance for parents and teachers to adopt a reasonably consistent approach in helping a child has already been established, and methods need to be discussed and agreed between them, so that at the very least each is familiar with the approach being taken by the other. There is sometimes a risk that the child remains for too long at a particular stage of development because it is assumed that subsequent delay is part of the handicapping condition. When development in severely physically handicapped pupils takes place in 'slow motion' or when it is distorted by the severity of handicap, it is particularly important to maintain a regime of demand and expectation, both at home and at school, which leads to teaching goals that are developmentally appropriate.

McConachie (1982) reminds us that 'further progress in developing services for young and handicapped children is crucially dependent on understanding, and respecting the range of different ways in which families think and live their lives. Approaches based merely on educational technology will fail to meet a child's or a family's needs, just as institutional answers failed previously. In the school situation, teachers must consider the needs of the whole child and not just his need to learn; they must build on their relationship with the child in order to teach him.' Similarly, Mittler suggests: 'parents are learning some of the technical skills of teaching, such as breaking a task down into small steps, using prompting, fading, and reward techniques and so on.' Partnership is of crucial importance in integrated education, and involves a two-way process of joint assessment and decision making in which parents and schools come together right from the start. Since the influence of the home is clearly fundamental, partnerships with parents should be considered a central component of special educational provision. It is obvious from the practical investigation that the range of relationships between parents and teachers is very wide. The range extended at one extreme from merely formal communication about dates of terms to open access to all reports and records on their child, at the other; from participation of parents in classroom activities to their involvement in discussions appertaining to school policy and curriculum development. The Education Act 1981 formalizes the rights of parents to be involved in decisions concerning their child's special educational needs. However, once the child is in school, collaboration between parents and teachers is a matter of good practice rather than legislation.

In four of the survey schools, it was policy for the headteacher and/or class teacher to visit the family at home, before the handicapped child began school, to get to know the family and to observe the child in his home environment. Such visits are an invaluable source of help for teachers to learn something of the child's behaviour at home, and to begin to build up a picture of his strengths and special needs, at the same time identifying the priorities of the family. One school, school *F*, suggested that the initial visit helped to identify the best ways for the child to start school, for example by periods of part-time attendance; the extent to which a parent might stay with the child; any special difficulties with regard to eating, toileting, medical problems and transport. School *H* suggested the aim of a home visit is to begin to discuss with the family ways in which home and school can establish a working relationship, and to make it clear from the outset that parents are welcome in school.

There was evidence of meetings held to discuss important educational issues which included further development and extension of integration programmes, changes in school policy and organization – class grouping for example; aspects of the curriculum, methods of teaching, and changes in services or legislation. In addition to meetings for parents as a whole, eight out of the nine survey schools provided facilities for small groups of parents of handicapped and non-handicapped pupils to meet informally. Indeed, five schools have excellent facilities for such purposes and this is important, given that it is essential for parents to feel welcome and comfortable when they visit the school. Many schools hold regular meetings to review the progress of each child with special educational needs, and some invite parents to attend to participate wholly or partly in such a meeting. Such meetings are particularly productive where schools have developed a detailed curriculum plan with recording systems which enable both teachers and parents to provide information on the child's progress in reaching specific goals. In three survey schools, parents are invited into school to see the child at various stages of a programme to teach a specific skill. The parent is involved in planning, and is encouraged to carry on some of the teaching at home. Emphasis on achievements rather than problems can provide a good foundation for partnership between parent, teacher and pupil.

A form of home–school notebook and diary which travelled regularly between home and school was used by six of the survey schools. In four schools, these are sent on a daily basis, and in the other two at the end of each week to provide the parent with an account of the week's progress. In all instances where such notebooks are used, the child is non-communicative, or has a handicap affecting communication. It is, however, essential that such notebooks are not one-way communications from teacher to parent, but encourage parental comment on the opposite page. Smith (1982) suggests that the home – school notebook and diary can serve three specific purposes. They can be used by the teacher and parent for general information, for specific communications and instructions, and for active collaboration on a joint teaching venture. Examples given include discussion of specific steps reached on particular educational programmes, methods of teaching, record of achievement in reaching a particular step, change of plan to attain specific goals, and progress reports in general. Progress reports vary greatly in frequency, style, organization and information content; from a few brief comments organized along 'subject' lines like a traditional school report to a detailed account of a child's achievements in attaining goals outlined in an individual programme plan. Schools *A*, *B* and *D* provided parents with a termly progress report, which commented upon different areas of the curriculum, but in the main, very briefly. Schools *G* and *H* kept a *progress file* for each child, which contained samples of work at each stage of development, and which parents could see upon request. School *I* produced an annual traditional report for all pupils irrespective of special needs, and schools *C*, *E* and *F* kept detailed accounts of the child's achievements at every stage of their individual programmes. For the purpose of meeting special educational needs, a report can provide an opportunity to step back and review progress, and reconsider priorities. Parents of handicapped pupils at schools *C*, *E* and *F* considered the accounts kept by the teachers as starting points or stepping stones for a joint approach to the development of further programmes of collaboration between themselves and the schools.

Promotion of parental involvement

When a large group of pupils with special needs are placed in a mainstream school, changes must occur within the school. Parents of non-handicapped pupils need to be made aware of such an important development in the life of the school, and reassured that the presence of the handicapped will not deflect on their own children's progress. If parents are involved from the outset, as in the case of seven of the nine programmes in schools in the survey, then they will generally support the idea and give positive assistance in a variety of ways. Ignorance can do a great deal of harm, but if fears are allayed, then good co-operation can be established. In several cases, the parent – teacher associations raised considerable sums of money for the purchase of specialized equipment, for building adaptations and extensions, and in three schools, parents' workshops were formed to assist in making aids and apparatus for both the handicapped and non-handicapped pupils. Here was a valuable resource in socialization for the two groups of parents, and the workshops were very well supported. Also, an opportunity for parents to offer special interests and skills to the school. Many parents wish to have a greater degree of participation in the development of plans and programmes for their own children, and there was evidence of parental participation in extra-curricular activities, school visits, curriculum activities such as swimming, cookery, craft, music and, in one school, parents ran the library. In one school, parents' coffee mornings were held on a weekly basis, and parents worked together to make items for fund-raising activities. In another school, parents ran lunchtime clubs, and several schools encouraged parents to help as classroom assistants on a rota basis. In schools *F* and *H*, the parents of each new intake of pupils are told about the integration programme at the initial parents' meeting, and some parents request that their child is put into a class with physically handicapped pupils. It is generally agreed that this is the way it ought to be.

The development of better working relationships between parents and professionals constitutes one of the most significant developments in special education during the past decade. Many examples of good collaboration have been reported, Mittler and Mittler (1982) write, and 'a whole series of reports from government, professional and parent bodies endorse both its principles and its practice'. Partnership between parents and professionals involves a full sharing of knowledge, skills and experiences in helping children with special educational needs to develop as individuals. A commitment to partnership rests on the assumption that children will develop and learn better if parents and professionals are working together on a basis of equality than if either is working in isolation. Families of handicapped children vary as much in their behaviours and attitudes as any other families – it is the task of professionals not only to recognize the distinctive and unique characteristics of each family but also to show respect in their approach to the family. In studying the families of cerebral palsied children, Hewett (1970) concluded that: 'families meet the day to day problems that handicap creates with patterns of behaviour that in many respects deviate little from the norms derived from studying the families of normal children. They have more similarities with ordinary families than differences from them.' Most parents of handicapped children also have normal children in their families and it therefore makes sense to harness the experience and expertise of parents in bringing up these children, and in knowing the needs and strengths of their handicapped children. This experience and expertise is essential in building the foundations for integrated education.

Typically, parents of children who are integrated provide both general and specific forms of support, in both medical and educational spheres. Amongst the sample group, there was clear evidence of parents acting as collectors of medical and educational details, liaising between professionals and making contact with supportive agencies. Parental 'back up' of a different nature included boosting the handicapped child's confidence, encouraging mobility and fostering independence, but parents' interactions with schools and hospitals differed greatly. The more assertive sometimes seemed to be acting as 'pressure groups' on behalf of their child, and in eight cases, parents intervened because they felt too little was expected of their child in the special school situation, and hence they insisted on mainstream school placement. One father remarked: 'The standard of education was abysmal.' Parents of a further 11 children objected to the way their child seemed to have been dismissed as unworthy of an education, by officials of one kind or another. One parent described how she was incensed that the placement decision about her physically handicapped daughter was based on a brief visit by the Borough medical officer to the child's home. It was necessary, she said, to be extremely persistent in order to obtain a recommendation for mainstream school placement. Three parents said their local primary schools had refused to offer a place to their handicapped children, even on a trial basis, and several other parents felt that information about the alternatives available to special school was often absent or inadequate, and that advice given by different professions was sometimes contradictory.

Seven survey schools indicated they invited parents to the school to discuss any particular problems presented by the handicapped child, and attempted through discussion to find ways to jointly work towards a solution. All the schools agreed that teachers found it helpful to discuss a range of matters relating to integration, with individual parents. The parents gave examples of issues in which the school had involved them, and these included school policy, organization and curriculum, and further developments being considered, relevant to integrated provision for special needs. Five of the schools in readiness for introducing integrated provision had asked the parents of the handicapped pupils about their preferences for receiving reports, information from the school, social and informal meetings that would interest them, contacts with school and visiting staff, and with other parents. Parents' evenings are normally held termly to discuss pupils' work and progress, and parent – teacher associations provide opportunities for social and educational activities. Four survey schools held termly meetings to provide parents with opportunities to meet visiting specialists such as physiotherapists, speech therapists and educational psychologists. In schools *C*, *E* and *F*, parents were able to come in at an arranged time to see their child receiving therapy and discuss how they might supplement the treatment received in school, at home. The same schools had a very good relationship with the educational psychologist, who was readily available to see parents with the headteacher and teachers, to discuss pupils' progress, at the school.

Assessment

A view which has gathered momentum during the last decade is one concerning the rights of individuals to information, and this has resulted in a profound feeling amongst parents of handicapped children that they should be informed, consulted and fully involved in any assessment of their child's needs and recommendations for the child's special education. An interesting comparison might be made by the suggestion that where 'segregation in secondary education has generally faded with the growth of comprehensive schools, so the pressure has increased for the education of more children with disabilities within the ordinary schools in preference to education in separate special schools' (Brennan, 1982a).

Parents felt their confidence in the various professionals involved with their handicapped child would increase if they were better informed, and helped to understand the critical and pertinent aspects of diagnosis and professional judgements. The certainty of early discovery and intervention needs to be markedly improved, in order to add quality in assessment. Brennan further suggests: 'It is becoming increasingly evident that the principle of the new approach rests in a more positive attempt to regularize the contribution of the different disciplines to the assessment process, and to place them in an appropriate educational frame of reference.' An unequal balance in the system of assessment for special education has resulted in children being assessed by professionals, neither actively engaged nor experienced in the education of children with special educational needs. So, pressure increased for multidisciplinary approaches to assessment, emphasizing education, and determined by the special educational needs of children, to which could be related the proposals for their education.

Assessments and decisions about what and how to teach the child with special needs require the co-operation of both parents and professionals. When parents are shown how to carry out certain physical exercises they must be given intelligible explanations about the reasons why these particular exercises are necessary. Schools *B*, *C*, *E* and *F* considered this a factor of great importance in integrated provision, to enable the child to achieve maximum independence. It is important therefore to strike a balance between helping parents to learn professional skills, while at the same time retaining their own sense of identity as parents. Clear emphasis however must be placed on the role of professionals as people with special training, in working with children with special needs, and as possessors of all kinds of specialized techniques. The majority of parents interviewed believed that once their child was placed in school, he would pass into the care of highly trained and skilled professionals, and for some parents it was a shock to realize that teachers, like themselves, often felt overwhelmed and unprepared for the opportunities for day to day participation in assessing the child's needs and in implementing daily programmes of collaborative work. It is essential, however, to keep such factors in perspective.

Three schools involved the parents in the assessment of their child's skills, abilities and needs, by the use of published developmental checklists. Two other schools had developed their own checklists and the parents provided valuable information based on their own knowledge of the child's behaviour. Schools *D*, *F* and *H* went through their checklists with the parents item by item, whilst schools *C* and *E* gave a copy of the list to parents and asked them to fill it in. Discrepancies between the assessments made by parents and teachers can form a productive starting point for discussion, pointed out one headteacher, and it was generally felt that it is not uncommon for certain behaviours to be more in evidence in one setting than another. For example, ten of the handicapped children in the sample group lived with only one parent, and in eight out of ten cases the single parent was the mother, who was in fact looking after the handicapped child largely on her own, with little help or support from other family members or from the surrounding community. In such instances where unsupported mothers have special problems, any related difficulties may well result in certain behaviours being exhibited by the handicapped child.

The frequency of parents being given opportunity to comment on the records and observations of teachers towards the end of any initial period of assessment was sought, before their implications, in terms of teaching, are considered by the survey school. In five cases, once the school had completed its initial assessment, usually at the end of the first term after placement, parents were given the opportunity to see and discuss the interim findings, to contribute their own observations, and to comment on anything which, in their opinion, gave a misleading impression of their child, and his special needs. The headteacher and staff of school *F*, for example, felt that full involvement of parents in the initial process of observation and assessment, and in the resultant formation of the individual child's programme, is of essential importance. At the same time, it is equally necessary for parents to share with school staff the methods that they have found helpful and unhelpful, in their own experience of the child at home. At this stage three headteachers commented: 'it is a good time to discuss ways in which teachers and parents are going to continue to communicate, and to keep each other informed about the child's progress, and further needs'. The initial period lays down the foundations for later collaboration and trust. Mittler and Mittler (1982) write:

> Collaboration between parents and teachers can take a very wide variety of forms during the child's years in school. The nature and quality of collaboration will vary with the changing needs of the child, the parents and the teachers. Relationships between home and school must therefore be flexible and must be able to respond to changing circumstances and the different responses of different families.

It is perhaps of much greater importance for mainstream schools meeting pupils' special educational needs to consider its policies and practices in relation to the development of partnership with parents.

In the past decade, parents have responded with great success to the opportunities provided by professionals to share in the task of working with their own child. This response has been particularly noticeable in programmes of integration and perhaps can be attributed to new developments in the technology of teaching, which not only lend themselves to communication with parents, but which lose much of their force if they are not shared with parents. No matter how successfully the physically handicapped child is taught in the mainstream school, the effort is largely wasted unless systematic steps are taken to help the child to use and apply his learning in his own home and in all the other real life settings in which he moves. The collaboration of parents is indispensable for this purpose, and the influence of a positive and successful experience of collaboration with professionals is examined in detail in Chapter 5.

4
In-Service Training

The teacher's understanding of special educational needs is important in relation to what is taught, and for the impact on attitudes and opinions towards integration. In Chapter 1, reference was made to the relationship between information about handicap and the attitudes and opinions held. Attention was drawn to the significant correlation between attitudes held by professional workers and their educational background or work experience, suggesting that the relationship between acquiring knowledge, and attitude modification, is far from direct. Conclusions were reached which indicated that those teachers who were currently involved with handicapped children were more likely to promote positive perception and attitude change in teachers, than teachers who did not have such involvement.

Information dissemination

Amongst the sample group of teachers, 58, the majority of those in the survey schools had relatively little knowledge about special needs, when the integration programmes began in their schools. Table 4.1 gives the distribution of responses to two questions relating to the nature of the handicapping condition, and information received to help understand the child and related problems.

Teachers involved with the physically handicapped child tended, generally, to assess the extent of their knowledge about physical handicap as reasonable, from the outset of the integration

programme, with a positive increase in the understanding of the
handicapped child and his relevant problems, during the first year
of the programme's operation.

Table 4.1   Initial knowledge of handicap

Non-existent	Poor	Reasonable	Good	Very good	Total
0	23	31	4	0	58

Table 4.2 gives the distribution of responses to questions relating
to the extent of satisfaction regarding information received after
first-hand experience of integrating pupils with special educational
needs.

Table 4.2   Subsequent knowledge of handicap

Non-existent	Poor	Reasonable	Good	Very good	Total
0	5	20	24	9	58

This reported increase in knowledge was attributed by teachers
to two sources in particular: direct experience of pupils with
physical handicaps, including many with associated learning
difficulties; through teaching thereof, and interdisciplinary
interaction, largely on an informal basis, with special education
advisers, educational psychologists, therapists and school medical
officers. The influence that a specialist facility can exert affects the
relationship between the support available to the mainstream
teacher, and the attitude subsequently held towards pupils with
special needs is complex. Whether or not the specialist facility sees
itself as having an advisory function, its presence alone provides a
basic reassurance which most teachers felt they needed.

Teachers' competence in handling and teaching pupils with
special needs involves numerous factors: general teaching skills;
perception of the pupils and attitudes towards them; the precise
nature of the pupils' needs; the teaching context and the kind of
support available. Those teachers in the sample group who felt
they had sufficient knowledge stated without any doubt, this was
only the position given the circumstances in which they found

themselves working. Such a statement is important, in that their estimates of the adequacy or inadequacy of their knowledge reflects two aspects. First, the existence of a specialist facility on site and its relationship with the host school, and second, the demands made on them as teachers in a mainstream classroom situation. In only one survey school, school *E*, was undue concern expressed by teachers about the extent of their knowledge, but in this school there was a repeated mention of the complexities of the various physical conditions, and of how these might affect pupils' educational development. However, there was some concern about the physical limitations that different handicaps imposed, and the need to counteract related emotional problems which some pupils displayed, in schools *B* and *F*.

The fact that some 70 per cent of the survey teachers felt insufficiently informed about pupils' special educational needs perhaps reflects a degree of isolation on the part of specialist and support staff, of whom it would be seem, there are fewer available as a resource for teachers in mainstream schools. Most teachers interviewed felt reasonably confident about their level of expertise with regard to the 'general course of teaching' but looked to special education advisory and support staff for advice and guidance for specialist teaching. Hegarty and Pocklington (1981) identified the precise role which mainstream teachers adopt, as being dependent on the degree of specialist expertise available to the school, and in their recent study, found a range of opinion regarding the importance of specialized knowledge of handicap. 'Teachers felt that specialized knowledge of handicap was essential or very important; desirable, somewhat important, or important in some circumstances; and not important' (Hegarty and Pocklington). However, this investigation revealed the majority of teachers working with the physically handicapped child considered it important to have specialized knowledge of the handicapping conditions. The headteachers of schools *C* and *E* emphasized how essential such knowledge was, for purposeful integration to be achieved, in view of the implications for teaching, imposed by the severity of handicap in relation to functional ability, and the degree of associated learning difficulties.

In all the survey schools, the headteachers had been involved in discussions prior to the integration programmes being planned, and in schools *A*, *D*, *G* and *H*, the programmes had been initiated in the first instance by the headteachers themselves. In all but two schools, *A* and *I*, the headteachers had fully involved their staffs, and parents of their pupils, in the initial plans for the integration programmes, and in all future developments thereafter. There was no evidence that any programmes of integration had been established in any survey school without the agreement of the headteacher and staff. The teaching staff of school *F* suggested that an essential prerequisite of any integration programme was a commitment to a belief in what they were doing, and a willingness to learn. There was a strong feeling expressed by the staff of school *H* that personal support and advice, ongoing consultation and opportunity to become acquainted with physically handicapped children, necessary in order to extend their own knowledge, led to confidence in integrated education. Jamieson *et al* (1977) suggest that 'if a child's admission to a school has a lot to do with the headteacher, the subsequent full acceptance of the child and his difficulties has much more to do with individual teachers'. Ideally, before any programme of integration is decided upon, all the staff of the school should be consulted and their views sought on accepting physically handicapped pupils into the school. They might then be advised as to what is entailed in the proposed venture, and how they, as teachers, might be affected by it. Information about the special needs that the proposed pupils have, the implications for lesson content and teaching practice, and the existence of outside agencies which can offer assistance, must, essentially, be given.

Attitudes

A number of teachers interviewed recognized that their teaching competence as far as pupils with special needs were concerned was limited. Twelve other teachers considered themselves insufficiently informed about the educational implications of given handicapping conditions and suggested they needed to develop their awareness of pupils' potential. Related to this was the problem of knowing what to expect of, and demand from, pupils, and how to handle untoward behaviour.

Special education in the past tended to stress the handicaps, disabilities and limitations of handicapped children and the results of this emphasis created a negative rather than positive attitude toward their education. However, during the last decade there has been a determined effort to look further than the preoccupation with handicap and behaviours. If teachers' opinions are based on such preoccupations, it is likely they will fail to see the behaviours that are constructively relevant to the learning processes. The headteacher of school *C* pointed out that if the handicap is allowed to become the focus of the child's life, it is unlikely that the best teaching programmes will be planned for pupils with special educational needs. The five members of teaching staff directly involved with the schools' integration programme suggested the basic motivation for affection, acceptance and approval exist for the handicapped child as for any other child. Furthermore, they stressed positive attitudes by staff were essential to security, and were firmly of the opinion that children with special educational needs might only be secure when accepted, understood and liked. Such attitudes complement Thomas's (1975) suggestion that 'understanding the handicapped child means first understanding him as a child, and only then understanding the ways in which his disabilities may influence his development and behaviour'. Pocklington (1980), in his article 'Integration – a lesson from America', pointed out that in a sample group of teachers in a mid-western American city, sex was the only variable significantly affecting attitudes, women teachers rather than male teachers being more favourable towards the disabled. This perhaps highlights the relative importance of changing teachers' attitudes if those of the public are to be changed.

The difficulties of logically distinguishing a group of pupils whose educational needs are 'special' from other children who nevertheless have needs particular to themselves which could equally well be described as special, have been summarized recently by Aspin (1982):

In a sense, special education is tautologous: insofar as we are dealing with children and intend to bring about increases in their perception and understanding of the world and ability to come to terms with it, there is no difference in kind between one sort of interpersonal transaction devoted to educational ends, and another. Yet, insofar as certain children do seem to need an extraordinary degree of care and attention, in order to counteract particular difficulties under which they labour, we can term such extra effort 'special' as being greater in degree, though not in kind, than what 'normal' children require.

Aspin points out that as teachers we approach problems in the field by a process of negotiation and in terms of our interpersonal judgements that serve to 'define the situation'. The notion of special needs contained in the Warnock Report rests on an educational judgement about the sort of provision which particular children require. These are judgements which will be made for the most part in mainstream classrooms by mainstream teachers. Teachers' opinions on the special needs of their pupils are therefore of prime importance.

The overall view of special needs as seen by primary school teachers which emerges from this survey gives support to the view that there is a consensual notion of the constitution of special needs upon which the contribution of mainstream schools and teachers in the area of educational provision is dependent. A recent research project, after studying a number of integration programmes, concluded that:

> Special educational needs can be met in the ordinary school, and to a far greater extent than is currently the practice. There are many pupils in special schools at the moment who could be educated satisfactorily in ordinary schools, given the requisite commitment and resources. (Hegarty and Pocklington, 1981)

This study emphasized the essential role of teachers in such a process.

Experience of 'special needs'

In the present practical investigation, consideration is given to the experience which teachers in the survey schools have had of handicapped pupils, how well they think they have met the special needs of these pupils, and to their attitudes towards the integration of severely physically handicapped pupils in the mainstream classroom. Eight teachers had experience of pupils who have moved from their classes into special education; 15 teachers had experience of pupils who had transferred from special education; 12 teachers had experience of pupils considered candidates for special education, but whose parents had resisted such placements, and there were numerous examples of the determination of schools and teachers to keep a particular child with special needs in the mainstream school. These factors suggest the sample group of teachers in the survey schools have some varied experience of pupils with special educational needs.

Teachers' attitudes to integration are often based on the practical experiences which the teachers believe they have had with pupils with special needs in the mainstream classroom situation. Croll *et al* (1982) suggest 'it is evident that the experience of having sensorily handicapped and physically handicapped children in the classroom was generally considered far more satisfactory than the experience of having ESN (M) or maladjusted pupils in the classroom'. In his conducted research, Croll found that in 80 per cent of all the cases of physical or sensory problems, the teachers said that they had coped at least 'fairly well' and in over 40 per cent of all instances of handicap, they felt they had coped 'very well'. In the present practical investigation, the teachers in the sample group were asked about their experiences with physically handicapped pupils in the mainstream classroom, and their response is shown in Table 4.3.

Table 4.3 Teachers' experience of pupils with handicaps

Poor	Fairly satisfactory	Moderately satisfactory	Very satisfactory	Total
4	14	24	16	58

It is of interest to note that these two sets of results are comparable, in that handicapping conditions which are not centrally relevant to problems of classroom learning and adjustment have given rise to the more satisfactory experiences. The teachers in the sample group were also asked how they would react to having severely physically handicapped pupils in their classes, with associated learning difficulties. The various responses are presented in Table 4.4 and it should be noted that teachers were not responding to the principle of integration, or to an ideally run integration programme, but to the notion of a multipli-handicapped child placed in their classroom, without major changes in staffing or other provision.

Table 4.4   Teachers' response to the notion of a multipli-handicapped child in class group

Handicap	Enthusiastic	Fairly favourable	Cautious	Reluctant
Cerebral Palsy	7	26	20	5
Spina Bifida	2	18	30	8
Muscular Disease	3	34	18	3
Other impairments	12	39	7	0

Seventy-five per cent of the teachers indicated that their views were more favourable to the principle of integration than their reactions to the specific instances might indicate. Some teachers pointed to the difficulties they were experiencing already, particularly when they were teaching large classes (schools *G*, *H* and *I*) or pupils from multicultural or socially disadvantaged backgrounds (schools *D*, *E* and *F*). Nine teachers felt that although they favoured the idea of handicapped children being in a mainstream school, wherever possible, they considered they personally lacked the training and expertise to deal efficiently with problems of learning difficulties and physical management related to handicap. One teacher from school *E* where a non-selective integration programme was in operation, pointed out that there were specific teaching difficulties when multipli-handicapped pupils were integrated: 'teaching materials must be structured appropriately, to meet their special educational needs, and necessary adjustments made to teaching approaches.' Another teacher from school *H* was of the opinion that a great deal of uncertainty amongst teachers related to the lack of advice and support available to the school. She thought also that when teachers have handicapped children in their classes, they are alerted to their own deficiencies in 'normal' teaching techniques, too. From these findings, two critical observations might be made. First, some forms of special need were seen as quite removed from the average teacher's experience and if teachers are to cope with them, they need a good deal of specialist support. Secondly, again and again, school staff reported having been denied access to information concerning the handicapped child, which might well have enabled them to meet special educational needs more accurately and expediently, on the grounds of medical confidentiality. Similarly, Hegarty and Pocklington (1981) concluded that 'the transmission of information in this area does raise particular problems, that medical personnel were not always minded to solve'.

Opinions relevant to the principle of integration

It would seem that what was more important than support for the idea of integration, was whether or not teachers were actually prepared to have physically handicapped children in their own classes and under what conditions. It is sometimes suggested that teachers' attitudes are likely to be a major obstacle to the integration of pupils with special needs in mainstream classes. Hence, in the present study, teacher opinions were sought, and altogether, the opinions are considered of 58 teachers working in the survey schools. Fifty-two were in favour of the integration of physically handicapped pupils, six were indifferent, and 45 of the 58 teachers who expressed opinions had pupils with special needs in their classes at the time of the study, or had had so in the recent past. Overall, it is encouraging to note such supportive attitudes, despite a small number of teachers expressing initial apprehension. However, such apprehension can be a barrier to the future development of integration programmes, given that all teachers are not equally willing, nor have positive attitudes towards the principle of integrated education. Jones (1980), writing about teachers' attitudes towards disability, points out that 'the threshold for acceptance of disability was found to be directly related to teachers' preferences and attitudes towards specific disability groups'. What her study indicated conclusively was that the special acceptability of all the children studied was not related *per se* to severity or degree of disability, to mobility or more tenuously to educational attainments. However, what appeared to influence children's acceptance by teachers was related, to a greater or lesser degree, to the children's own personality characteristics, their level of social adaptability, and more particularly to their level of educational attainment, associated with severity of behavioural difficulties.

An identified source of tension amongst the sample group of teachers was the choice that staff felt they were forced to make between wanting to normalize the child's presence in school, by not extensively modifying his environment or programme, or segregating the child in any way, and wanting to ensure that the child did receive requisite attention and that proper allowances were made. Attitudes amongst teachers in seven of the nine survey schools towards integrating physically handicapped children were very positive; nevertheless, there was stated evidence of considerable apprehension from both headteachers and teachers about integrating physically handicapped pupils, when the integration programmes were first suggested, particularly given the number of teachers who had had no contact with handicapped children. As Foster (1975) points out, a school may be ideally advantageous logistically, but what must be more importantly taken into account, as an absolute priority, is the individual and group attitudes of those people who will be closely associated with the pupils with special needs. The headteachers of eight of the nine survey schools were fully supportive of the inclusion of physically handicapped children in their schools, given that their respective integration programmes had enjoyed a considerable measure of success. The headteacher of school *C* voiced the opinion that she had 'accepted the direct responsibility for giving to the staff the support and confidence that is essential if pupils with special needs are to become full members of the school'. 'The teaching staff have a responsibility for promoting physical and social opportunities for physically handicapped children to work and integrate with confidence, within the classroom situation': headteacher of school *E*; and 'at the same time ensuring that the non-handicapped pupils do not have the classroom programme changed to their detriment, in order to accommodate a small number of pupils with special needs': headteacher of school *I*.

Apprehensions

A small number of teachers in the sample group, six in total, expressed reservations about integration, although they were not unwelcoming to individual children with special educational needs. In schools *C, E* and *F,* which operated non-selective programmes of integration, several teachers cautioned that there was a need to judge each physically handicapped child on his own merits, and ascertain what he could achieve at the school, rather than adopt wholesale a programme of integration for all pupils with special needs. In contrast, the headteacher of school *H* declared herself and her staff willing to take children with any sort of handicap. She considered integration to be ethically, socially and educationally right and desirable, an opinion shared by five of the class teachers, approximately 50 per cent of the staff.

It is of interest to compare the findings of this study with those of Moses (1980). In examining the perceptions of both head-teachers and teachers, Moses found that headteachers were much more hesitant than the class teachers about both the desirability and the practicality of integration. All the headteachers in Moses' study thought that integration would impose severe strain on their staff and the handicapped children would take up a dispropor-tionate amount of teacher time. They saw many practical problems that would be difficult to overcome – access to buildings, stairs, toilets, and the problems of breaks and other activities where handicapped children could not join the others. As one head-teacher stressed, 'We've got problems with the children we already have' and generally speaking the headteachers were of the opinion that many of the pupils with special needs would require medical care and specialist teaching of a sort that most teachers could not provide. Headteachers did not relish the implementation of the Education Act 1981. But the reactions of class teachers, Moses found quite different. Generally, they were in favour of having as many handicapped children as possible in mainstream classes, and although the teachers considered ancillary help in the classroom would be useful, they did not regard this assistance as essential. They did indicate, however, that additional help at playtimes, dinner breaks, etc. would be welcome. The teachers felt the handicapped children would profit educationally and socially, and that their presence would have a good effect on the non-handicap-ped members of the class. They regarded 'caring' as being of prime importance in their job, yet seemed unaware that as well as being cared for, many of these children needed to be taught using specialist techniques outside the repertoire of the average primary school teacher.

Cannon (1975) carried out a careful study of attitudes, which suggested the main anxiety expressed by mainstream teachers was whether they were fully meeting the needs of the physically handicapped child, the general assumption at that time being that the quality of provision and teaching would be better in a special school. Teachers in mainstream classes need more than information; they need, especially, confirmation that they are doing the best for the child. Cruickshank (1981) suggests that 'the significance of the disability – so the handicapped children tell us, is impressed upon them by the adults who surround them'. Teachers as educators are the factors which make integration succeed or fail, who:

> determine the degree to which we imprint the disability as a matter of consciousness on the mind of the child who happens to own the disability. We accentuate their minority status by typology, by attitudes, expressions, emotions and by other forces which draw children to us in a healthy way or repel them from us, and make them isolates (Brennan, 1982a).

There is a necessary basic minimum of knowledge required by all teachers on the staff of a school hosting an integration programme, which, together with visits to appropriate special schools, should form an essential induction course and promote the beginnings of positive perceptions by teachers towards integration. Generally, teachers in the sample group considered it an essential prerequisite to receive some form of preliminary in-service training and advice from specialists, before embarking on full-time classroom integration. The first essential of a programme of integration for physically handicapped pupils in the mainstream school is the qualified and experienced teacher, and Cruickshank further suggests that:

> positive attitudinal characteristics toward disability are a necessary prerequisite, and such attitudes can be achieved by including in basic teacher training and subsequent in-service training courses, the development of handicapped children and their psycho-educational needs, providing for the future teacher, a positive basis for teaching children with special educational needs.

It cannot be taken for granted that teachers will, in the majority, welcome an integration programme. Outright opposition is rarely found, but hesitance and ambivalence can certainly be expected.

Where teaching staff are concerned, each survey school regarded as a matter of significance the fact that they were given early information about the proposed programmes of integration, and hence made to feel involved in the programme from the outset. Staff of the school who are not directly affected need to develop a commitment to the integration programme, as an integral part of their school. One teacher from school *B* admitted to feeling uncomfortable in the presence of physically handicapped children and she found some repulsive. There was evidence in two schools of over-protective attitudes, resulting in teachers being reluctant to treat handicapped pupils like their peers and make comparable demands on them. This tendency appears to be most pronounced with severe physical impairment, where mobility is very restricted and teachers are fearful of children's safety or the harm of over-exertion (schools *B* and *D*). However, plans to involve the two ancillary assistants in the weekly PE and games sessions in school *D* meant that the physically handicapped pupils would be able to participate in part, but school *B* felt as they had not been afforded additional staffing resources for their handicapped pupils, they should not, as a matter of principle, compromise.

The few initial negative reactions observed during preliminary visits did give place to more positive attitudes by the end of the study programme. One teacher from school *F* confessed that she could not cope emotionally with the demands of integration which had resulted in fearful apprehension. She confided that she had been prepared to resign rather than have a physically handicapped child in her class, but after voicing her fears to the headteacher, she had been reassured that she need not be directly involved in the integration programme. One headteacher who was doubtful about the wisdom of accepting pupils with special needs in her school agreed, reluctantly, to place a cerebral palsied child in her school for a trial period. Following a very successful 12 months, she voiced enthusiastic comments about the benefits for all concerned, in understanding and dignity, and agreed, without any hesitation, to admit a spina bifida child to the school. The staff of school *B* had strong reservations about a programme of integration, involving pupils from an adjoining special school, which had begun very successfully and operated for a year, unless they were given special school allowances, extra welfare assistance and better staff – pupil ratios. The headteacher supported her teaching staff, and hence the programme was severely restricted. The programme has since been increased, but the criteria for admission to it is that the physically handicapped pupils must be able to walk! This has resulted in parents requesting transfer for their children with special needs to other primary schools in the borough, whilst others have been denied access to a mainstream school education. The lack of support given by the LEA in this matter has caused further problems and generally exacerbated the situation.

Factors influencing attitude change

There are a number of factors which may effect a positive change in the attitudes of the teacher towards pupils with special educational needs. Baker and Gottlieb's research (1980) refers to five components of teachers' attitudes towards integration:

(a) knowledge of pupils' academic and social behaviour;
(b) feelings about their own competence to teach them;
(c) expectations of receiving support;
(d) beliefs about the advantages and disadvantages of different placements;
(e) general educational attitudes.

Other factors, they suggest, are the prevailing attitudes towards the disabled and minorities in general, and the self-perceptions of non-disabled groups within society at large. There is clear and positive evidence amongst the sample group of teachers in the survey schools, to suggest that modification of attitude amongst teachers led to a realistic acceptance of children with special needs in the mainstream school. Such attitudes of acceptance on the part of the teachers also clearly influenced the non-handicapped pupils in the direction of realistic acceptance of their handicapped peers, and this aspect will be discussed in greater detail in a later part of the chapter. The survey finds the most effective results are obtained when programmes designed to encourage positive development of attitude are presented in conjunction with actual experiences. This general pattern of association accords with the results of other studies such as the NFER integration study (Hegarty and Pocklington, 1981) and the University of Leicester

School of Education pilot study: assessment and incidence of special educational needs (Moses, 1980). A similar conclusion might be drawn here; teachers' initial reluctance and uncertainty about integration programmes have generally given way to a more positive response, following experience of the programme in operation.

Supportive services

The headteacher of school *E* takes the view that 'integration is a growing movement which depends in the final analysis on belief which is based on sound practical judgement, and that judgement depends on the establishment of effective communication'. The teacher of the pupil with special needs is committed to that child each and every day. In order to adopt a positive attitude towards working with the handicapped child, and to be able to perceive some of his related special needs, it is vital that a teacher can feel confident about clear channels of communication between the various agencies involved with that child. The involvement of the medical services, the LEA, social services, education welfare officers, advisory and support staff and the headteacher, will ensure each child with special needs will benefit from the shared expertise of the professions. It can not, nor should be implied, however, that all communication will aid attitudes of acceptance. Communications need to contain information – understandable statements about factual matters. One headteacher felt the *medical model* could not always be understood; another suggested the *academic model* asked questions rather than gave answers, and one teacher in charge of an integration programme expressed concern that communications could seek to destroy what information people may already have, rather than add to it. So, the factual content of the information provided is important as such information might usefully offer solutions to classroom situations, present explanations that are understandable, and reduce anxiety and apprehension amongst teachers involved directly with the integration of handicapped pupils. Generally, comments from teachers in the Sample Group verified the absence of any coherent system for ensuring that information is communicated effectively to all relevant parties – specialist agencies and class teachers. Another area of difficulty indicated was the lack of time for liaison and support.

The individual headteachers of six survey schools passed on their knowledge, information and insights to their respective staffs, but in the remaining three survey schools, there was some evidence to suggest that this did not always occur. Indeed, the headteacher of school *I* forcefully expressed the opinion that 'the more information the staff receive about the handicapping conditions, the more problems they (the staff) find when teaching these children with special needs'. There was little evidence of organized in-service training, but in schools *E* and *F*, headteachers arranged for their schools to be closed for one day's in-service training per term. The staff were addressed by experts in the education of handicapped children; special education advisory and support staff, educational psychologists, school medical officers, physiotherapists and speech therapists, headteachers of special schools, to name but a few. Staff had a chance to voice concerns and fears, and generally gain an understanding of how the handicapping conditions can affect the pupils' performance in the classroom. One particularly useful and positive aspect was the invitation by schools *A*, *B* and *D* to headteachers and staff of schools already integrating pupils with special needs to talk about their experiences. As the headteacher of school *D* pointed out, 'teachers will always listen to other teachers'. Preparation of school staff might also be the responsibility of special education staff, advisory and support teachers. One advisory teacher's policy was to give colleagues a minimum of detail so that they would not be put off by the difficulty of the task. In her work with staff in schools *H* and *I*, she felt it important to 'tell them generally what they need to know...don't inundate them with details, it is essential to elevate the classroom teacher, to foster positive opinions and perceptions'.

Before the integration programme began, the headteacher of school *C* made several visits to existing programmes of integration in mainstream schools for pupils with special needs, in other boroughs, as well as local special schools where the pupils were placed. She discussed practical issues with a wide range of practitioners with experience of teaching the physically handicapped, and searched out relevant literature. She arranged opportunities to discuss and share the knowledge she had gained, and the insight she had acquired with members of her staff, as well as encouraging them to air their anxieties and concerns. In addition various teachers visited special schools, and some went on DES courses involving developments within special education, at local colleges and teachers' centres. In a neighbouring borough, an integration programme was established linking a school for the physically handicapped with the adjoining school *B*, sharing the same campus. Here preparation remained largely in the hands of those most closely and actively involved, and the aim was to work towards special needs pupils' assimilation into the mainstream school, and foster feelings of competence amongst the mainstream school staff. A teacher with responsibility for liaison between the two schools was appointed one term before the first pupils were integrated. Time was spent with the headteachers, and teachers of the classes where the handicapped pupils would be placed, giving information, seeking to reassure, clarifying the intentions of the venture, answering questions, and arranging for those members of staff who were interested to spend some time at the special school. Two matters considered crucial were getting across the notion that mainstream teachers had a definite contribution to make – 'let them feel they are partners', and having special school teaching staff accompany integrating pupils to lessons in the early days of the programme.

In order for in-service training to have a positive influence, teachers must be receptive to the various ideas and opinions which will be expressed by the different agencies involved. A small number of teachers in the sample group were perceived to be too limited in the ways they thought about, approached, and reacted towards the physically handicapped child. In two LEAs where physically handicapped pupils were placed individually in their local schools, schools *A* and *G*, by arrangement between headteacher and parent, there was no initial induction, or in-service training of any kind – a major limitation of the programmes. In school *H*, where there had been little initial planning and no briefing of either the headteacher or staff, the headteacher took it upon herself to read around the subject and communicate basic information to her staff. In a number of schools, the mothers of the handicapped pupils were a valuable source of information concerning medical and management aspects and in two schools, the community physician was of valuable assistance in both supplying information and introducing supportive agencies to the school (schools *E* and *F*). However, when information is supplied in such an *ad hoc* way, gaps in information communicated can exist, and there is a danger of misperceptions and incorrect handling procedures being passed on.

Baren *et al* (1978) remind us that there are numerous components in the role of the teacher meeting special educational needs. They suggest that 'Their job can be complex and demanding and in terms of daily routine and professional demands, very different from that of the average classroom teacher.' Monitoring the progress of pupils with special educational needs, and recording it systematically, should be an integral part of teaching activity. The teachers' involvement in case conferences, where they can make a positive contribution to the assessment of pupils' progress, is of significant importance, yet at only three of the survey schools, *C*, *H* and *I*, were such conferences held regularly, and only the teachers of schools *C* and *H* were invited to attend. Occasional case conferences were held at the divisional education office, for pupils with special needs attending schools *E* and *F*, but at these conferences the views of the individual class teacher were represented by the headteachers and teachers-in-charge of the integration programmes. Yet, it is essential to establish good liaison and communication between all agencies concerned with the provision of education for pupils with special needs, in the mainstream school. Frequently, different groups concerned with their own particular services to children, can unintentionally create pressures, by failing to share a practical appreciation of the aims of integrated education, and the common problems experienced. The survey established a very real and urgent need for effective communication, particularly between the schools and the respective district health authority services 'theoretically' available for pupils with special needs. The majority of the staff in every survey school expressed grave concern at the lack of positive help from specialist agencies, and the deterioration in interest shown by LEAs, once the integration programmes became established.

5
Interdisciplinary Interaction

The preceding chapters of this section have examined in detail the role of parents and teachers in integration, and discussed the relevance of expectation and attitude, and the influence of opinion and perception. This chapter seeks to determine the importance of interdisciplinary interaction, and identifies the need for adequate services, psychological and medical diagnosis and treatment, and the expert psychological, social and educational support for the teacher, child and family which is necessary throughout school life. The role of professional personnel in the school psychological services, the LEAs and the community child health services is examined, in relation to the integration programmes studied, and their attitudes towards interdisciplinary interaction, which might be seen to influence the successful integration of pupils with special educational needs, are discussed.

In working with children exhibiting special needs, professionals often bring differing perspectives to the task. These perspectives can be a source of strength in developing educational programmes, or they can represent a source of conflict with resultant misinterpretation in communication, and even hostility. This can be avoided, however, if each party understands the other's perspective. The problems which arise when the school placement of a physically handicapped pupil is either being considered, or supported, are frequently seen differently, by the various professions involved. Each specialist is likely to emphasize different needs and to envisage different kinds of practical problems. It is these projected problems which cause the parents most anxiety, and the attitudes of the professionals are liable to influence the final choice of schooling which parents select. Some of these aspects are therefore now discussed, which relate to the problems experienced by parents of physically handicapped children, with regard to school placement.

LEA organization

Physical handicap is, in the first instance, the concern of the medical profession; it receives first notice of individual cases and, in conjunction with health visitors, makes initial contact with the handicapped child and its family. Hence children who may well require special educational provision are usually brought to notice by the district health authority services, and there can be considerable involvement on the part of the community child health service. While formal assessment and recommendation for school placement are the province of the school psychological service, the medical service makes a major input to placement decisions, either informally or through participation in case conferences. The school psychological service is involved in programmes of integration primarily through its formal role in initial placement. Individual educational psychologists conduct assessment on children referred to them by the medical services, as requiring special educational provision. The decision on school placement depends, not only on physical handicap, however, but also on the child's mental abilities, and social and emotional factors. The schedules for the Education Act 1981 state that the proposed new statement on children with special needs should be based on educational, psychological and medical advice, thus ensuring that the assessment of the child's needs is multiprofessional.

Multiprofessional assessment of children's educational needs was recommended by the Warnock Committee, endorsed by the Education Act 1981 and is generally accepted as desirable. However, Mittler (1979) states this is largely 'lip-service' and Tomlinson (1981a) comments that recommendations for multiprofessional assessment such as those made by the Warnock Committee assume an 'unrealistic degree of communication, co-operation and absence of professional conflicts and jealousies'. A more sensitive matching of needs to provision must be encouraged by separating the assessment of needs embodied in the educational, psychological and medical advice given in Part B of the Education (Special Educational Needs) Regulations 1983 (statement of aims), from the specification of provision in Part C. The draft notes of guidance underline this distinction, emphasizing advice offered by the professionals to the LEA for the purposes of statement, 'should not be influenced by considerations of the eventual school placement' as in the past. The practical investigation revealed that some professionals, especially psychologists, fear conflict between their desire to advise freely on the child's special needs, and the influence exerted by the knowledge of the provision currently available. To avoid such conflict, it is essential that members of the professions have the united support of their colleagues, in order to justify their recommendations. For example, three of the survey schools suggested that conflicting advice from the specialist agencies encouraged LEAs to hold placement meetings at which provision for pupils with special needs could be considered. The special education adviser to schools *E* and *F* felt that professionals from all disciplines concerned may need, on occasion, to press for team and placement meetings, in order to ensure informed and considered decisions about provision. However, the educational psychologists for schools *C*, *E* and *F* considered that the annual reviews of children for whom statements are maintained will, if conscientiously done, be useful measurements of success or failure in terms of the chosen special education provision.

School *H* described how, once integrated provision for physically handicapped pupils was established, LEA officers, and the special education adviser, who had played a central role in the establishment, retreated into the background. As a consequence, staff felt isolated and unsupported, and although a few were satisfied to be left to develop the programme without specific advice, most would have welcomed a continuing indication of interest and support on the part of the LEA. By contrast, in an effort to sustain initial impetus, after opening a new provision in school *C*, the LEA set up a steering group of professionals with relevant experience to monitor the operation of the integration programme and to contribute to its further development. The group consisted of the principal educational psychologist, the senior advisory teacher, the community physician (child health) and the teacher in charge of the special resource class. The advice given to the school related to two different aspects: advising on teaching and planned curriculum areas, and advising on organizational and operational matters. With regard to teaching and areas of the curriculum, the LEA had a good staffing level, and the senior advisory teacher had a substantial degree of involvement with classroom teachers on a variety of matters – acquiring specialist resources, both learning materials and technical aids to learning; informing teachers of new developments, and promoting in-service training through experience.

Interprofessional consultation

It is rare for multiprofessional assessment in special educational procedure to include direct consultation between the members of the professions concerned. In the normal course of events a pre-school or school age child with special needs will have access to a range of professional help. Within the school, for example, this range will consist of the skills of the classroom teachers, the help of resource teachers, and visiting specialists such as speech therapists, physiotherapists, school medical officers and nurses, visiting advisory teachers, educational psychologists and advisers for special education. These personnel may give direct assistance to the child with special needs or through consultation with the teacher. The practical investigation indicated, albeit on a small scale, that the availability of such resource personnel varied, and did not always meet the perceived need. The nature of help available to the child with special needs depends on the level of 'good practice' locally.

It is relevant to examine the process of assessment and admission to the special resource class, in order to identify the importance of the role and attitudinal influence of specialist agencies. Any children with special educational needs can be referred to the special resource class in school *F*. The nature or degree of the handicap is evaluated once a need has been perceived, and in fact the present classification system in special education is seen only as part of the process of determining how much the observed disability actually handicaps a child. Referrals to the special resource class come from a variety of sources, such as local primary teachers, GPs, the county advisory service, parents or the schools' psychological service. The referrals are processed in a systematic way, and each child is seen for full psychological testing and assessment by the educational psychologist and social worker. Parents attend, observe their child being assessed, and are considered essential to the assessment. They are made fully aware of, and helped to understand, the extent of their child's strengths and weaknesses, and hence a working partnership between parents and professionals is established. Such a partnership can influence the parents' attitude towards their child, and help them to become aware of the implications of the handicapping condition, with regard to his education. Test findings and implications are shared with the parents and staff in the special resource class, and full medical information is obtained from the medical officer. The staff then spend time observing the child, on a trial basis, in the class, or in his own teaching group, if already placed, and discuss his educational progress with the specialist agencies involved in the assessment procedure. This information is collated and presented to the admissions support team for discussion, and if placement is considered appropriate, the staff invite the parents of the child to discuss what the special class can offer the child, and to answer any queries.

The special resource class operating in school *F* is the pivot of an *area scheme*, the object of which is to detect children with handicapping conditions, and children who are educationally 'at risk', as early as possible, thus ensuring that the maximum number of pupils with special needs are educated within the mainstream primary schools of the area. The scheme, which is described more fully in the following part of the chapter, is supervised by the area educational psychologist, and the special resource class teacher, based at school *F*. Case conferences, in-service training and parental involvement are part of the co-ordination initiative, and direct school support comes from advisory teachers, therapists and the school medical officer, with occasional support from education welfare officers and social services. Organization for children with special needs at primary level rests in vertically grouped mixed ability classes working an integrated day, in both schools *E* and *F*. Children with special educational needs begin in the special resource class, after their fourth birthday, and are fully integrated into mainstream classes as soon as the area support team feel they are ready. Their teachers are then supported by members of the area service who withdraw pupils for specialist help and therapy, where necessary, in both schools. At primary level the progress of pupils with special educational needs rates as very satisfactory, and by the very nature of the organization their social interaction is continuous throughout their primary education.

School psychological service

During interviews with headteachers and teachers, both were asked about their interaction with the school psychological service. Opinions about the usefulness and relevance of the service varied to a great degree. From the evidence of the small sample of survey schools, it would seem that the headteacher had the most contact with the service. The educational psychologist to schools *E* and *F* suggested that the headteacher establishes the school's relationship with the service, and the general attitude towards it. The opinions of the headteachers about the school psychological service, however, albeit varied, in every case echoed the feelings of the staff. The amount of contact was variable, and, on the whole, the more contact schools and teachers had with educational psychologists, the more favourable was their impression. Four of the nine survey schools reported the liaison as very favourable; three, the liaison as favourable; and schools *G* and *I* said they had very little contact with the service, and certainly felt that a significant lack of interest was shown towards their integration programmes.

Problems in practice

Schools *C*, *E* and *F* were enthusiastic about the help given by the educational psychologists. This help was described in the form of testing, diagnosis of educational problems, suitably adapted programmes for the child in the classroom situation, and frequent visits to monitor the progress of pupils with special needs and to discuss these pupils with the staff concerned. Often the psychologist recommended additional ancillary help in the classroom, to that provided by the LEA. The teaching staff claim that the advice given by the psychologists is practical, relates directly to their work in the classroom with pupils with special needs, and that it can be carried out without undue strain. The expertise of the psychologist is regarded with some esteem by these three schools, who appear to make advantageous use of the service. At the same time, such expertise clearly influences the positive attitudes and perceptions which the staff of the schools have towards integration. In contrast, school *G* was only vaguely aware of the existence of the service, and had virtually no contact at all. Fortunately, the physically handicapped pupils integrated into this school present no problems in learning whatsoever, according to the head-teacher's comments, and so, in this case, liaison was not essential. As the headteacher stated, however, both she and her staff would have welcomed some interest in their achievements with the pupils with special needs.

The headteacher of school *I* was less than enthusiastic about the school psychological service. He found they could rarely, if ever, offer constructive advice. When he did make contact with the service it was usually to try to ensure extra help for a child experiencing learning difficulties, or to secure a change of placement if a child with special needs was failing, educationally. The headteacher thought his school could cope with all but those pupils with severe learning difficulties associated with physical handicap, and that these pupils should be placed in a special school. The psychologist rarely visited the school, unless specifically requested for a particular reason, and showed, according to the headteacher, little interest in pupils with special educational needs, once they had been placed. On rare occasions case conferences were held when important decisions had to be made, and the psychologist agreed to become involved at such times.

The headteachers of the four other survey schools were all reasonably satisfied with the help they received from the school psychological service. Although they agreed that, on the whole, the help of the educational psychologist was valuable, one headteacher pointed out that there was often much too long a gap between the school's referral and the child being seen. The headteacher of school *H* felt that frequently the schools, the psychological service, the medical services and the social services appeared not to know what each other was doing – in short, interdisciplinary liaison was absent, and this could cause great confusion in some cases, leading to individual members of staff feeling they could not adequately meet a pupil's special needs. In order to understand a teacher's difficulties, emphasized the headteacher of school *B*, the educational psychologist must be prepared to spend regular periods of time in the classroom, in order to observe the pupils with special needs, and, where necessary, to appreciate their individual problems. Otherwise the recommendations made by the psychologist might not be suitable for the teacher to undertake in the individual classroom environment. To make additional special provision for individual children was often not a practical reality, and hence the role of the educational psychologist in integrated education was virtually diminished.

Stages of successful integration

The educational psychologist to schools *E* and *F* suggested that his work involved three separate stages as far as successful integration was concerned. First was the preparation of the school and its staff, followed by the preparation of the handicapped child and his family. This latter preparation will be further discussed, in detail, in the following section. The importance of preparing the non-handicapped pupils and their families was also stressed here. The second stage involved the introduction of the pupil with special needs to the school, to the staff, and the individual teacher, and to his non-handicapped peers. This stage, suggested the psychologist, could be achieved gradually on a part-time basis, before proceeding to full-time integration. The third stage, the psychologist considered perhaps the most important, was the monitoring of the child's social and emotional adjustment and subsequent educational progress, once integrated into the mainstream school environment. Sorting out initial problems, and closely liaising with staff to give support and advice as necessary, were of extreme importance if integration was to be a successful venture, he pointed out. School *C*'s educational psychologist described how she attends 'information evenings' for parents of next term's new pupils, to talk about the pupils with special needs, emphasizing that parents have an important task to perform, to give their children a positive outlook on their handicapped peers. She visits the school regularly to talk to the headteacher and staff, and makes herself readily available, to spend time with individual teachers, to discuss special needs and any resultant difficulties which arise. Case conferences are arranged by the psychologist as and when required, and before handicapped children are admitted to the school, she talks to the classes where they will be placed, about handicap, and shows a short film. Children have the opportunity to ask questions and a visit is sometimes arranged to the special school or class, to meet the handicapped children. The psychologist insisted, however, that it was important to ensure the visit is as simple and as natural as possible, so that it would not be considered an unusual event, to arouse curiosity.

In each of the nine survey schools, referral after initial placement was an unusual procedure. As was mentioned earlier in this section, two pupils had been re-referred and transferred to residential special schools; in another school, one pupil had been reassessed for placement in a day special school, and another was to be referred for assessment for residential placement. In a campus school situation, two pupils had been reassessed for transfer to their local mainstream schools, and in one other school a pupil with special needs had been reassessed before moving into another authority. When placement has been made there is usually no further involvement, either in the way of curricular guidance or reviewing of progress, the result of the pressure of work on a poorly staffed service. Although all the survey schools had contact with, or access to, an educational psychologist, 'usually over-worked and under pressure from many sources', suggested the headteacher of school *A*, after one visit early on when the integration programme has first begun, subsequent contact is generally on an informal basis, when the psychologist is visiting the school for other purposes.

Advisory and support services

Brennan (1982a) reminds us that it is essential that an advisory and support service should be established in any LEA where there is to be large scale expansion of integrated provision in mainstream schools. He suggests that the major objective requires that the placement of handicapped pupils in the mainstream school, responsibility for reviews of their progress, teacher establishment, allocation of scale posts, establishment of non-teaching staff, provision of equipment and capitation allocations should be the responsibility of the assistant education officer for special education. The special education department must accept responsibility for planning integrated provision in mainstream schools, as part of the new wider concept of special education. Such continuity of management responsibility is necessary to establish and maintain comprehensive special education provision. The task requires close consultation with assistant education officers for primary education, and there will be many points of contact with other public services. Of particular mention is the development of positive working relationships with community health services. Efficient co-operation is therefore essential, and the inspector/ adviser for special education will be the main professional adviser to the assistant education officers in relation to specialist provision. Hence a situation is created where there is an input into the mainstream school for the benefit of the handicapped pupils, which is over and above the general entitlement of the host school. Yet, in only two of the LEAs which this practical investigation was concerned with, did such a situation exist. Ideally, the situation so described should encourage the acceptance of pupils with special needs, by the mainstream schools, and provide interaction within them.

Diversity of role

Bolam *et al* (1978) noted considerable diversity amongst those employees of LEAs engaged in advisory work and how they were styled. The practical investigation revealed the reflection of this diversity in special education. Two of the four LEAs employed an adviser specifically within the area of special education; two employed advisory teachers who were specialists in a given field of special need, but not the physically handicapped, and in two LEAs there was no adviser for special education but an assistant education officer whose remit was special education. Three LEAs employed a principal educational psychologist, two of which had an advisory function, and such appointments were highly successful. Hegarty and Pocklington (1981) suggest the work of the advisory service is to advance an LEA's provision at two levels: that of the school, and that of the authority. It aims to stimulate, advise and evaluate educational activities in schools, and report on the same to the authority. Many features of the advisory role are applicable to special provision, and a major feature is the appointment of staff to work in integration programmes, involving new recruitment and deployment of existing staff. Apart from appointing or participating in appointing staff, as was the case in eight of the nine survey schools, advisers also had a concern for determining staffing levels, creating a career structure and providing motivation and encouragement. In five survey schools, staffing ratios were deliberately enhanced to take account of the demands of integration, and classes with physically handicapped pupils were smaller.

According to Bolam, advisory staff typically face a tension between the professional and administrative aspects of their role. They face in two directions simultaneously – towards teachers and schools, and towards policy makers and administrators. In their professional or advisory role, they try to improve educational standards through their advice to teachers and schools and, reciprocally, they advise policy makers and administrators about the needs and problems of schools and teachers: 'the attempt to give equal priority to both produced intolerable role strain' observed Bolam *et al* (1978). Two of the LEAs with which the practical investigation is concerned had in post both an assistant education officer and an adviser with responsibility for special education. The other two LEAs had one or the other, and their involvement of officers tended to be administrative rather than advisory. The investigation found sparse involvement of the advisory staff with the day-to-day running of the integration programmes, which was clearly dissatisfying to the teachers involved, yet justified by the advisory staff on the grounds of priorities and other calls on their time. Although visiting schools occupies a good deal of an adviser's time, visits to any given school are rarely part of a regular cycle. Hence, it can be reasonably assumed that the survey schools could not rely on a regular commitment from the advisory service, despite the many requests from teachers for such involvement. Whilst two advisers did have a special education background, the assistant education officers with responsibility for special education in the four LEAs had no such background and hence were unable to offer positive and constructive advice to the schools and their integration programmes. This is all very well when experienced advisory staff are in post with the requisite experience and skills, but as Hegarty and Pocklington (1981) point out, 'Where there are no specialist advisers, however, not only must the administrative function predominate, but it runs the risk of not being informed by the expertise that a specialist adviser would bring to bear'.

Advisory teachers

One LEA had attempted to minimize the lack of expertise by creating more advisory teacher posts which had potentially given career opportunities to staff from special schools and units, while enabling their specialist expertise to be used more widely. Three LEAs appointed teachers in a support role to assist handicapped pupils in lessons in the mainstream school, which enabled them to follow the main school curriculum. This was one way of providing the necessary specialist expertise for the mainstream teacher. Teachers from the local special schools for physically handicapped pupils sought to help pupils with special needs in schools *B* and *C*, through their class teachers, by drawing up programmes of work specifically geared to the needs of the handicapped pupils, for implementation by the class teacher, using some of the learning resources developed within the special school. The specialist teacher visited the mainstream school regularly, and discussed progress each week with the class teacher, before agreeing further tasks and work assignments. Two specific areas of difficulty had arisen, however, in that three of the teachers in the sample group had assumed the responsibility for the special needs pupils was the specialist teacher's, and four other teachers indicated feelings of resentment at the specialist teacher's apparent interference. What appears to be an essential requirement here, of the specialist teacher, is the finding of a balance between helping mainstream teachers to develop their skills in teaching pupils with special needs, and giving the impression that they themselves have all the answers.

It is suggested that the aim must be directed towards the joint development of plans of work involving specialist and class teachers, initially, but allowing the class teacher to gradually assume responsibility for setting the weekly objectives, in order to provide the individual pupil assistance necessary. Implementing an integration programme, and monitoring its development, requires specific skills of liaison and administration, and it is of interest to examine how two survey schools carried out the implementation. Schools *H* and *I* gave responsibility for liaison for such a programme of integration to two senior teachers with appropriate scale posts, one from each school. The campus special school for physically handicapped children appointed a teacher to accept responsibility for liaison, and he had a substantial amount of time set aside for this work. Staff of the three schools were informed of the arrangement and asked to raise any matters concerning a pupil with special needs or the integration programme, with the appropriate liaison person, in the first instance. Much of the time was spent in attending to administrative details, and all three headteachers were actively involved in such matters, resolving problems and anxieties amongst staff and pupils, dealing with special aids and equipment, and keeping the same in working order. The liaison teachers were involved, generally, in ensuring that pupils with special needs were benefiting from integration provision, and in the formal assessments of pupils' progress. They participated in discussions about placements, met regularly with all members of staff involved in the programme to discuss any difficulties which were arising, or any concerns which they had, and to generally give encouragement, and plan future development. It is relevant to mention the view of the liaison teacher for school *H* who considered that interpersonal skills were at a premium in this kind of work, and were perhaps more important than the possession of specialist expertise. Of critical importance is the ability to relate effectively to colleagues and enlist their co-operation, in order to resist uncoordinated development of integrated provision, which offers little security to the pupil with special needs. Personal qualities identified as being essential to the role of liaison teacher were ability to establish positive working relationships with others, by encouraging discussion and joint agreement; willingness to listen to others' viewpoints, rather than pushing a personal point of view; having a respect for protocol and the authority to make decisions, and tactfulness and patience.

Therapists

The survey schools in the practical investigation varied considerably in the amount of help they received from medical and social services, but only three schools had direct interaction with speech therapists and physiotherapists.

Speech therapists

Five schools found speech therapists helpful in giving advice on specific techniques or programmes to promote language development amongst pupils with special needs, and used them a great deal in an advisory capacity. But, there was much dissatisfaction, particularly in schools *B, H* and *I*, about the extent of the provision of speech therapy. Speech therapists visited these schools at intervals ranging from once per week to once per term, and their visits were not considered to be frequent enough to meet the children's needs, particularly bearing in mind the fact that these therapists were 'on-site' on a daily basis, at the adjoining campus special schools. From observation, it is reasonable to assume that these therapists were not entirely in favour of integration. School *G* had had great difficulty in getting an assessment for one of their special needs pupils, with an obvious speech difficulty.

Physiotherapists

The provision of physiotherapy for pupils with special needs in the mainstream school is a major problem, and in order to make improvements, a more constructive approach must be adopted, a view generally expressed by teachers in the survey schools. Amongst the sample group of physically handicapped children, it was apparent that ten children would benefit from regular physiotherapy, but did not receive it. Only three of the survey schools provide regular treatments, two others can arrange physiotherapy if absolutely necessary, but to suit the physiotherapist rather than the child, and four have no facilities provided. In three cases, the parents pay for private treatment out of school hours. Ten years ago, Anderson (1973) drew attention to the fact that district health authority personnel often insisted a physically handicapped child attended a special school, in order to receive therapy. This view posed a question as to whether educational or medical matters be given priority, and my own study revealed that some ten years hence, this question was still posed. The community physician (child health) with overall responsibility for schools A, B and D, agreed that admission to mainstream school was a 'first priority' for children who were physically handicapped, but that 'continuity of physiotherapy was an objective of nearly as much importance'. Such an attitude poses an obvious dilemma for parents and schools.

The physiotherapists working in school C are full-time members of staff, and so treatment timetables are worked out by the headteacher, in consultation with the therapists and teachers of pupils with special needs at the beginning of each term. Every physically handicapped pupil receives regular physiotherapy or hydrotherapy treatments, and the ancillary staff are fully involved in all treatments, and hence assist the therapists as aids. Regular internal case conferences are held with the class teacher and ancillary, headteacher, speech therapists, physiotherapists and school nurse, and occasionally the school medical officer and parents. At such conferences there is full and frank discussion of any problems which have arisen and the sharing of advice on various aspects of care. The pupils' educational achievements, social, and emotional adjustment, are also discussed. Under direct supervision of the physiotherapist and school nurse, the ancillary staff take responsibility for the seating and standing arrangements for the child within the classroom, the adaptation of aids and specialist equipment, and the maintenance and repair of the same, and for all toileting arrangements and trainings. From discussions with both teaching and ancillary staff in school C, it was obvious they were acutely aware of the physical needs of their pupils, and well advised and equipped to meet such needs. The staff have a good understanding of their pupils' conditions, and are building up appropriate skills in dealing with them. Attitudes are positive, with no evidence of over-protectiveness, and it is obvious that the pupils with special needs have much to gain through having a normal school experience.

COMPONENTS OF THE PHYSIOTHERAPIST'S ROLE

The main components of the physiotherapist's role identified were: treating individual pupils; training, and working with, ancillaries; and monitoring equipment. The balance between these will reflect the individual pupils' needs, but a key factor in programmes of integration is the amount of delegation involved. It is noted from the findings of the practical investigation that delegation is necessitated by the number of pupils to be seen in a limited period of time, and the extent of the severity of handicap amongst pupils. The regime in schools E and F is for the physiotherapist to assess every pupil with special needs when they enter the school, to work with those pupils requiring regular treatments, on an individual basis initially, and later, in both the classroom and general school context. In consultation with the teacher and ancillary assistant, the physiotherapist will assess any problems of physical management that the pupils present, and any difficulty with mobility, particularly in the classroom situation, and in the participation of class group activities. She then offers advice, and suggests practical solutions for any anticipated problems, and liaises closely with school staff, as and when difficulties arise. School F pointed out that it was particularly beneficial to have the advice of the physiotherapist as part of the practical assessment of new admissions; it was crucial, they felt, to be advised of any problem likely to be experienced in physical management before the pupil with special needs actually arrived. Preparation, the staff felt, was vitally important. In the classroom situation, for example, the physiotherapist concerns herself with assessing such issues as what would be the best form of movement, taking account both of pupils' mobility and obstruction to others, and sitting in on PE lessons is regarded as particularly crucial, to advise on routines or activities the handicapped child could cope with using existing or perhaps additional equipment. During her treatments of pupils with special needs, the physiotherapist will develop programmes of specific reinforcing exercises which the ancillary staff are able to carry out on a daily basis, and at times to minimize disruption of the pupils' education.

Ancillary staff

It would appear that many parents and teachers are unaware of the continuing importance of physiotherapy, and the lack of services provided by district health authorities is a major weakness of the integration programmes examined in this practical investigation. The general impression gained was that pupils' needs in respect of toileting, mobility and physical activity, and equipment maintenance, were poorly met, in consequence. The physiotherapists working on a sessional basis in schools *C* and *F* have involved the ancillary staff in routine treatments and exercises to ease the situation. As the number of physically handicapped children integrated and needing regular physiotherapy increased, the physiotherapists invited the ancillary staff to 'sit in' on some sessions, and explained what they were doing and why. The ancillary staff then took sessions themselves, working to the physiotherapist's detailed instructions, in their presence, so that they could correct as necessary, and offer advice for improvement. Given time, the ancillary staff have taken responsibility for specific exercises worked out by the therapist, and given extra treatments at times least disruptive to the pupil and teacher. Although further time for sessions for the physiotherapists are being considered for both schools, this present arrangement does relieve the pressure on the therapist services, and allows more time to be spent treating the more complex cases of handicap. Ancillary staff working in schools *H* and *I* are given a general introduction to the skills involved in routine treatments, where possible, some training at the campus special school, and then carry out the work in the specialist's absence. Such programmes of work are specifically devised for implementation by ancillary staff, and are regularly monitored by the specialist.

In school *E*, there were too few physiotherapy treatment sessions allowed to provide for all the physically handicapped pupils in need of therapy. Accordingly, the therapists gave the classroom ancillaries specific exercises to be carried out daily with individual pupils, in between the therapist's weekly visits. These exercises ranged from simple walking exercises or practising transfer from a wheelchair, to the fitting of splints and calipers to achieve independence of mobility. In addition, ancillary staff were asked to observe how a child was progressing physically, how he responded to treatment, and whether the treatment was appropriate. They observed difficulties experienced by the child, and noted signs of bad posture, limps, pressure sores, and, generally, the apparent worsening of the condition. The pupils with special needs integrated in school *B* were required to return to the adjoining special school for physiotherapy. This arrangement was fully approved of by the headteacher and staff of school *B*, although not by the parents of the pupils concerned, who felt physiotherapy should be given in school *B*, at a time to suit the child. It might be noted that such an arrangement precludes liaison of any kind between the teachers and ancillary staff, and the physiotherapists, and hence professional interaction is severely restricted.

Parental involvement

Placement procedures differed somewhat between areas and individual schools and classes. In seven out of nine cases, the child with special needs is referred to the school, by a specialist agency, and teachers and parents are involved in placement decisions to a varying extent. In the three cases of physically handicapped pupils being placed in special resource classes, the professional agencies concerned discussed the placement initially with parents, who were invited to discussions at, and with, the school. The majority of teachers in the sample group, 80 per cent, were satisfied with the procedures for assessing, and placing, pupils with special educational needs, in their classes, but there were obvious barriers to full communication involving specialist agencies, as described earlier in the chapter. From the replies of the headteachers of the survey schools, five were reasonably satisfied with placement procedures for pupils with special needs. With regard to the initial placement of handicapped pupils, there was most involvement on the part of the professional agencies, particularly school medical officers, in schools *C*, *E* and *F*. Schools *A*, *D* and *G* accepted children at the request of their parents, without any formal placement procedure, and schools *B*, *H* and *I* accepted pupils with special needs on the recommendation of the headteachers of the local special schools, but occasionally met with interference from the district health authorities, when such placement was resisted. This interference, they observed, made the persistence of the parents of the pupils more acute. Table 5.1 shows the level of satisfaction with placement procedure – discussion, assessment and decision making.

Table 5.1 Satisfaction with placement procedure

Response	Headteachers (N=9)	Teachers in Sample Group (N=58)
Very satisfied	2	37
Moderately satisfied	3	11
Not satisfied – no discussion with professional agencies	4	10
Total	9	58

Table 5.1 suggests that there is some room for improvement in both groups, in connection with placement procedures.

None of the professional agencies concerned escaped criticism. The headteacher of school *I* commented: 'children are often placed before discussions take place. The apparent procedure of admitting after professional panel discussions, is not adhered to.' Another pointed out that a multidisciplinary approach to admissions is not adopted, and rarely were parents involved in group discussions prior to entry (school *H*). The headteacher of a campus school, school *B*, said she never had any contact with other professional agencies, but had to rely on the campus special school headteacher as the link between the school and specialist services. The general feeling conveyed was that unless there was adequate and appropriate multiprofessional interaction, it was impossible to ensure that the acceptance of severely physically handicapped pupils and those with associated learning difficulties, would not have an adverse effect on the school's ability to cope with those pupils with special needs already in the school. The headteacher of school *C* stressed the importance of determining that the handicap was sufficiently severe to preclude acceptance by the mainstream school, of the pupil with special needs. Although schools *A*, *G* and *H* indicated by their replies that there was, to a great extent, discussion and liaison between parents and schools, there was no active involvement of any external specialists – a situation not to the liking of either the headteachers or their staffs.

It is not unreasonable to suggest there is some diversity of opinion amongst the survey schools with regard to interdisciplinary interaction. On the one hand, considerable dissatisfaction was expressed by schools at the lack of guidance and support from specialist agencies, and on the other, the role and attitudinal influence of specialist agencies, within the integration programmes, was clearly visible. Staff in schools, and parents, were not looking for specialist training courses so much as basic instruction and access to expertise when necessary, and, it must be noted, that uncertainty on the part of otherwise experienced teachers resulted from a sense of isolation. Teachers were most aware of the educational consequences of their lack of expertise, but deficiencies, which the lack of interdisciplinary interaction draws attention to, must be acknowledged to be significant drawbacks to the integration programmes. Yet it is of interest to note that programmes of integration which had developed in a piecemeal and casual way, often in the absence of specialist personnel, were entirely successful in the education which they provided, for their pupils with special needs.

How essential are supportive services?

There are many specialist agencies that have a role to play in special education. However, it is not uncommon, as the practical investigation showed, for teachers to be unaware of the existence of specialists who could help greatly in meeting the needs of some of their pupils. The teaching staffs of schools *A, D, G, H* and *I* worked in considerable isolation, with only very limited guidance from external agencies such as special education advisers, educational psychologists and school medical officers. Multidisciplinary interaction is far from common and even where it exists, rarely is the teacher involved, as was discussed earlier in the chapter. Yet the inclusion of supportive services is particularly critical. In order that the teaching of pupils with special needs is effective, school staffs must have basic information concerning the handicapping conditions, and the likely implications for education. Schools should therefore be aware of agencies within the wider community, to whom they might turn for advice and assistance. The educational psychologist for school *C* pointed out how necessary it is to adopt measures to counteract negative staff attitudes which arise as a result of misinformation and misperception.

Those professionals who support the teachers and parents of a child with special needs in the mainstream school have the opportunity, when contributing to the child's assessment for 'statement' purposes, to make a case for additional help for him. They will continue working with the child, while the question of extra help is being considered. When a decision to make provision is reached, they will be able to continue their support if extra help in the child's school is the outcome, or they will be able to pass on their views about the child's needs directly if he is placed elsewhere. The external support available to the special resource classes in schools *E* and *F* includes a weekly commitment from the educational psychologist, and from the social worker, who has links with the local child guidance clinic, as and when required. The school medical officer is available for advice consultation, assessment and forward planning, in relation to the transfer of pupils with special needs to more specialized provision. In programmes of integration which are initially non-selective in recruitment, regular commitment and assessment by specialist agencies is vital, to ensure the child's special needs are being met, and to ensure a smooth transition to more specialized provision, if necessary. A successful working partnership between school and parent, and the specialist agencies is clearly evident in schools *E* and *F*, and has resulted, during the practical investigation, in the transfer of four of the pupils from the Sample Group to more specialized provision, with full agreement by all parties concerned.

Seven out of the nine survey schools reported no positive liaison with school medical officers, and in just two schools was there evidence of medical staff briefing the school in detail when each physically handicapped child was first placed. But this lack of liaison meant that there was virtually no information for the school, about possible educational implications, and no opportunity for the class teachers to become familiar with the various handicapping conditions. Consequently, there was a distinct danger of initial problems relating to the physical handicap, remaining unresolved for considerable periods of time, and becoming more problematic, as time progressed. Whilst many positive comments were made about the professional agencies, the general consensus of opinion from the survey schools was that liaison with such agencies was grossly insufficient, and hence neither positive nor constructive, in relation to the future development of programmes of integration. The following comments are relevant to this statement:

'Regular links with community health visitors have been requested, but there has yet to be an improvement in the service' – headteacher, school *B*.
'The health visitor used to supply a great deal of valuable background information about our handicapped pupils, but we have no such close contact with them now they are attached to GPs' – teacher, school *E*.
'Social workers change too frequently in most cases to achieve continuity, and have no appropriate training for special needs pupils' – teacher, school *F*.
'Advice is always welcome, but the specialist agencies appear not to want to advise us' – headteacher, school *H*.
'Once the school agrees to place a handicapped child, all that the future entails appears to pass from the LEA to the school' – headteacher, school *G*.

Gliedman and Roth (1981) capture the essential spirit of professional interaction: 'The need for services...dominates the concerns of many thoughtful parents and professionals.' Their belief that in spite of the advances of the past few decades, 'every handicap service needs to recast its conception of the proper relationship between professionals and clients in terms that honour the dignity and humanity of the handicapped child and his family' sums up, aptly, the findings reported throughout this study. The research of Hegarty and Pocklington (1981) came to the conclusion that it is essential for all specialist agencies, involved with pupils with special needs, to monitor programmes of integration in action, through observation and first hand experience. This will not only ensure the programme is on target and see that objectives are being met, but will allow account to be taken of emerging developments. The findings of this survey suggest that the need for involvement of external agencies must be critically examined and adequately identified, if there is to be a wholehearted commitment to integration. Baker and Gottlieb (1980) drew similar conclusions when they wrote: 'disproportionate availability of supportive services to special education teachers can hardly be expected to increase regular teachers' acceptance of integration.'

6
The Learning Environment

The requirement by the DES (1982a) that a child's special needs should be identified in terms of his educational requirements, has a number of virtues. Not least, that of focusing more attention on the classroom as a learning environment, rather than the belief that placement of a child in a particular school or group, on the basis of some assumed measured relationship with other children, guarantees integration to occur. McCall (1983) believes the stating of children's special educational needs, in terms of required educational tasks and an appropriate learning environment, calls for 'knowledge on the part of the teacher, drawn from many sources, and skills as varied in range as the needs of his many pupils'. There must be clear understanding of child development and the ability to organize a classroom to offer flexible learning opportunities for different levels of development. The ideal arrangement focuses on the classroom as a social group, and a multifaceted learning environment, particularly in relation to children with special educational needs.

The programme for the development of children with special educational needs is interdisciplinary. Most of the development required, for example, an increase in adaptiveness, in social as well as intellectual skills, in perceptiveness of relations and subsequent empathy, are the kinds of qualities and abilities that emanate only from a balanced curriculum and the experience of differing classroom groupings. The essential basis for human development centres upon the principles and techniques of social interaction, and a satisfactory curriculum is a matter of extending understanding of, and skill in implementing, learning environments of many kinds. Common sense plays an equal part with experimental findings in attempting to make specification of need classroom-based. The Education Act 1981 implies radical development towards broader assessment procedures, and in making sure that such procedures relate to the stated intentions of curricular activity. Such demands require the formulation of certain objectives, with subsequent responsibilities accepted. The school must have a philosophy around which a total programme of attack on the associated problems of special needs can revolve. A learning environment must stand for something, and must relate to the needs of its pupils. 'A professional staff', Cruickshank (1981) tells us, 'consistent and unanimous in its adherence to the philosophy and goals of the school, is essential'.

Classroom-based resource approach

Provision for handicapped pupils in mainstream schools must be developed against a variety of backgrounds. Unless there are clear objectives and priorities, circumstances will override principles. In integration, the objective is clear – it is to provide a varied and flexible system of alternative educational situations which will match the known range and variety of needs in every group of handicapped pupils. In schools *C*, *E* and *F*, the system is required to be capable of meeting the range of pupils' needs not only within any single handicap, but also to make possible the placement of pupils with more than one handicap or disability. And it must be sufficiently flexible to match the changing needs of the handicapped pupils as they develop and mature. If pupils with special needs are to gain socially and personally from interaction with their peers in mainstream schools, then the priorities should rest on the basis of curriculum and teaching. School *C* defined four interrelated elements of curriculum development: the setting of objectives; the choice of materials and experiences; the choice of teaching and learning methods to attain the objectives, and the appraisal of appropriateness of the objectives; and the effectiveness of the means of achieving them.

'Pupils who have special educational needs highlight the right of all pupils to an individualized curriculum' (Wilson, 1981). This can only be a reality if implemented via clearly defined teaching intentions, related to the use of classroom resources and group opportunities. Some Schools Council Projects, for example *Concept 7-9* and *Language for Learning*, planned for pupils in mainstream schools, show some of the features which are particularly appropriate for pupils with special needs – emphasis on the children's own activity and environment, learning by direct experience, relevance to pupils' interests and a thematic, rather than a subject, approach. Hence, breadth and balance in the curriculum are measured by how broadly each subject or topic is treated. The relationships between classroom groups, and intellectual, language, and social development must be closely interrelated, for education is concerned not just with the acquiring of particular facts or skills, but with wide-ranging and broad areas of development.

Trial teaching

For many pupils with special needs, the assessment of their learning difficulties, learning style and strong learning channels is not an easy or short-term affair. An effective assessment procedure, and one adopted by school *C*, because of its availability for application in a variety of group sizes and settings, is the concept of trial teaching. The main value of this concept is that it encourages the teacher to adopt the approach of contributing directly to the child's assessment, identifying difficulty and need in essentially curricular terms and adopting a *research* orientation to the learning problems of individual children. The Bullock Committee (1975) indicated that it is probably the most effective way of assessing learning difficulty and progress. Trial teaching involves grouping children for part of a day by classroom sub-groups or cross classification procedures, in order to conduct more systematic teaching, using a variety of lesson materials. The application of this concept in school *C* was via routine classroom arrangements, indicating an awareness of the diagnostic-prescriptive teaching angle on the part of the teacher and the school.

Translating the aims and methodology of curricular experiences into classroom programmes that meet special educational needs requires a great deal of conscious thought. To design specific classroom-based activities that interrelate developmental activities, and offer experiences which form a continual sequence of individual and social development, is a masterly task. The real issue centres on the continual and ongoing examination of the total atmosphere of the school, because the total school environment is a group structure that meets, or does not meet, the needs of pupils with special difficulties. Judging from the replies received from the practical investigation, schools support the view put forward by Rutter *et al* (1979) that the behaviour and performance of individuals are directly influenced by the school's atmosphere, this being created via its ethos, emphasis, and styles of organization and management. Special educational provision within mainstream schools exudes its 'hidden' curriculum as much as any other educational institution. However, such a curriculum, McCall suggests, 'might indicate little "specialness" despite the fact that, outwardly speaking, the buildings, resources, written curriculum guidelines, staffing ratio and staff expertise are good'. The systems analysis approach to special needs problems in mainstream and special schools, suggested by Bailey (1981), offers a broader diagnostic framework than traditional methods. A 'systems' appraisal incorporates reviewing institutional organizational influences that may impinge on a child's performance, as well as considering factors within the child himself (Burden, 1978).

Programming to meet individual needs

Barton and Tomlinson (1981) suggest a *resource programme* undertaken in a mainstream school describes a room or rooms, staffed by a teacher or teachers with specialist qualifications, and an ancillary assistant, and specially equipped according to the needs of the children. The primary emphasis of this 'approach' is on programming to meet individual needs, rather than grouping children in categories of handicap. The guiding principle is that all children's educational needs should be met as far as possible within a mainstream class within a mainstream school, and so the resource programme is developed as an integral element in the total curriculum and organization of the school. The special education provided is conceived of primarily as an instrument for the facilitation of change and the development of better ways of meeting the learning needs of all children, not only of those who are deemed to be different (Jones, 1981). As a model the 'resource approach' requires that special education becomes an adaptive system that is responsive and relevant to the needs of all children and not only for those children defined as different by categorized criteria. Such an approach highlights a fundamental issue of the special education debate, namely, that the problems confronting both special education and mainstream schools are those which are intrinsic to education in general – how to educate those who are difficult to teach. The major task in applying the 'resource approach' is to find ways of helping teachers, advisers, specialists and administrators to look at familiar problems in new ways, and adopt new attitudes to recognize that there are no satisfactory cut-off points in a range of educational opportunities.

The headteacher of school *C* sought a method of working which involved substantive contact between the school staff and children outside special education. She envisaged the school making a contribution to the broad group of children with learning difficulties, associated with various physical handicaps, and instigated the development of a specialized curriculum in basic literacy and numeracy. Staff, in turn, were encouraged to specialize in one particular curriculum area, such as language or reading, so that the school was able to take an area of special need, whether learning difficulties, English as a second language, or physical handicap, concentrate on developing the area as a resource, and then provide a comprehensive curriculum. At the start it was realized that any additional contribution the school was to make towards meeting special needs via the resource approach would require a favourable staffing ratio, and this was provided. The result is a highly formalized curriculum, jointly developed by a number of staff. In each of the four areas of mathematics, reading skills, language development, and fine motor co-ordination, the staff have produced graded materials along a developmental sequence. Special needs pupils at a low level in basic skills all follow a broadly similar curriculum, though they differ in their point of entry for any particular area. A behavioural objectives view was also adopted, materials were produced to provide each step in a learning chain and individual pupils progress was systematically charted (Appendix E).

Curriculum design

The primary school child has a need for present satisfaction, and fulfilment in expressive and creative work. Fundamental skills are important, and a balance has to be achieved between direct skills teaching and all the varied activities which widen horizons, arouse interest and give purpose to learning. It is essential that the class teacher planning a school day sees balance as the need to ensure a varied range of activities. This balance and variety is of critical importance in the education of pupils with special needs, and their needs should be met equally in the fields of intellectual, emotional, social and moral development, which necessitates much greater freedom of timetabling and grouping arrangements. Currently, moves towards curriculum integration, flexible social and academic grouping, and curriculum-based assessment are creating new roles for teachers and making new demands on their skills, whilst establishing firm foundations for fundamental provision for pupils with special educational needs. In its introduction, the practical investigation found examples of team teaching, resource-based learning, which involved elements of individual and self-study, particularly appropriate for pupils with special needs, and increasing evidence of teacher involvement in assessment by profile, and in keeping records of personal achievement. Mixed ability teaching was evident in seven of the nine survey schools and this required ongoing development and classroom-orientated support, opportunities for developing insight and imagination amongst pupils, and teaching programmes structured to promote initiative. Schools *B* and *I* have highly developed academic programmes, and perhaps could extend their scope for developing practical skills. Too much time spent on basic skills may bring diminishing returns, since skills develop best when put to use, a factor so clearly illustrated by schools *C* and *F*.

Aim analysis

Schools *B*, *C*, *D*, *E* and *F* analyse, and set out their aims, in writing, and make it part of their work to assess regularly how far the education they provide matches these aims. This practice is in line with a direct recommendation of the DES document *The School*

Curriculum, a document which stresses the importance of establishing terminal and immediate objectives for each branch of study. In classroom practice in the survey schools, it has been found helpful to set up specific short-term objectives in each subject, for each child, favouring objectives in behavioural terms, which indicates what the pupils will be expected to work towards, after each level of achievement. Schools *B*, *D* and *H* stress the need for clear statements of objectives as an invaluable feature in relation to meeting special educational needs, since such pupils have greater than normal need for short-term objectives and quick feedback. School *E* believes it essential to identify what is expected, so that classroom work can be adequately planned, recorded and evaluated. Hence, a well-planned, written curriculum ensures that the principles of continuity and progression are maintained, and team work amongst teachers in developing an overall plan is considered of vital importance.

Responsibility for the curriculum is vested in the headteacher, yet emphasis is being laid increasingly on the need to see the curriculum as a whole, and this makes it highly desirable that curriculum planning is a corporate exercise involving the whole staff. In six of the survey schools, this was the procedure, and after information had been gathered, discussions then took place involving the staff who, from their knowledge of the children, identified their needs. The special interests and expertise of each member of staff were also discussed. The headteachers of schools *C*, *E* and *H* sought the views of parents as to what they considered priorities, and the outcome of the various discussions resulted in a clarification of what the function of the school was to be, and what its main aims were, in relation to its special purpose. Attitudes, teaching methods and content of the curriculum are relevant to the fulfilment of aims, and it is essential therefore that some measure of agreement should emerge as to what skills, attitudes or areas of experience are necessary, which are optional, and what might be excluded. Only then is it possible to identify what main subjects or experiences are essential for all pupils in the school.

Objectives within each subject area

In the essential areas of the core curriculum, it is particularly important to be precise about the objectives within each subject area and how these relate to the main aims of the school as a whole. It was necessary at this stage, in four survey schools, to look closely at the situation within the school – the range and diversity of the pupils' special needs. The relationship between the essential curriculum areas and the existing expertise of the staff was also explored, so that any gaps could be taken into account in the planning process. Once the essential core curriculum has been identified, it is necessary to decide what proportion of teaching time can be devoted to it, and what should be reserved for other valuable experiences to be made available for some of the pupils all of the time, or for all of the pupils some of the time.

Six schools decided upon a broad range of compulsory subjects for all pupils, and the proportion for options was a quarter or less, whilst the other three schools adopted a core and periphery model, and hence the core was smaller. The core is for all pupils whereas other activities may be included in the curriculum to meet the special needs of pupils and to give them the opportunity for exercising choice.

An important aspect of planning is the setting of immediate objectives which mark stages in the pupils' progress towards final goals. Developments in task analysis have facilitated the matching of tasks to the individual needs of the children. 'It is essential, in the curriculum', points out one school, 'to clearly state what the pupils are expected to be able to do after a given period of instruction, so that both pupil and teacher have a better chance of knowing whether or not progress is being made'. The teacher with special subject responsibility has the task of selecting appropriate materials, books and equipment, of advising other members of staff on the setting of short-term objectives and on methods to be adopted on reaching these objectives. The purpose of curriculum planning is to achieve purposeful activities in the classroom, and actual classroom practice. Such planning highlights the differences between pupils, as well as involving the modification of objectives and methods, in the light of individual needs. There is considerable scope for variety related to teacher preferences, coupled with the strengths and weaknesses of individual pupils.

Social growth, development and change is not possible without a degree of conformity which allows for continuous social evaluation and criticism. These very subtle and often conflicting objectives require a careful balance between personal freedom and social conformity. Curriculum design contributes to the balance, but it is also achieved by teachers individualizing their teaching methods to take account of the personal needs of pupils, while using communal methods to promote social interaction, understanding and maturation. The conditions which determine individual handicap, generate personal needs at once more extensive and more complex, than those presented by non-handicapped pupils. To meet the extended personal needs, teachers individualize tuition to a greater extent, in a smaller teaching group, and advantage is taken of a combination of specialized resources and support services, accumulated in selected areas. In one Home County, the high cost of providing for handicapped pupils in the mainstream school is reduced by concentrating the necessary specialized facilities within selected mainstream schools to which pupils with special needs are transported. Thus, schools *E* and *F* provide for physical handicap, within one division, and this allows for the provision of specialist facilities at lower per capita cost, and a concentrated input of supportive services. Such an arrangement keeps catchment areas to a manageable size, and provides for the maximum integration of handicapped pupils with their non-handicapped peers.

Curriculum areas

All aspects of the humanities, whether treated separately or as integrated studies, can be treated with more depth and complexity as the pupils increase in age and maturity. Such aspects are considered to be of essential benefit in programmes of integrated education, and can be ideally approached through areas of first-hand experience rather than separate subjects. In the education of physically handicapped pupils with moderate learning difficulties, the aims should be personal adequacy and social competence, and schools *D*, *E* and *F* have achieved this through the subsidiary aims of building up self-confidence, self-knowledge and good work habits. Classroom work is directed towards the improvement of self-image, the arousal of interest and increased understanding of feelings and behaviour. So, the interrelationships which become evident give support to the subjects of the integrated curriculum, which is particularly favourable in schools meeting pupils' special educational needs.

The effectiveness of the range of activities must be measured and recorded so that the pupils with special needs are assured of an appropriate education programme. Only through the utilization of several techniques can the evaluative system be effective and enhance motivation and learning. This is so, because the essence of group activities and experience is broad development, and narrow evaluative procedures are likely to restrict the programme and suggest to the participants an inadequate representation of abilities. The need for curricular activity to embrace broad areas of experience, and enhance concepts, skills and attitudes is essential. Evaluation must become appreciative judgement, that is, judgement informed by both measurement and qualitative devices, and by professional and non-professional opinion. Classroom materials and activities must be re-emphasized as the main channel of evaluation data. McCall (1983) believes that sources of 'within learning' material and 'within learning' procedures offer excellent opportunities for assessing areas of intellectual and social development equal and beyond those offered in formal testing and assessment procedures. Brennan (1982b) takes the view that the education of children with special educational needs presents a tension common to all education in democratic societies. Democratic education has a continuing aim of fostering the greatest possible personal development for the pupil, and socialization, in a manner acceptable to his society.

School *F* produced its own reading scheme which concentrates on developing a sight vocabulary of 150 words before moving on to phonics. Besides 30 reading books, there are flash cards, tapes and numerous word games involving 'characters' from the books, and staff ensure that each child has mastered each new stage in a number of contexts before moving on to the next stage. Worksheets, books and games are stored centrally, and produced in a form in which they can be easily replaced and reproduced. There is a strong emphasis on child-centred individual education, and a salient visual feature is that the individual educational plan and monitoring system for each child in each basic skill area is pinned on large boards in each resource area. The special resource class and the two classes containing the youngest pupils organize their days in a similar way. The mornings usually involve a varied use of the highly structured core curriculum in basic skills. The afternoons are used for freer activities – projects, creative work, mime and movement, etc. The four classes of older infants have basic skills work more closely integrated into their curriculum as a whole, and at the centre of their education are a series of interdisciplinary courses.

Team teaching

The staff are committed to team teach the jointly prepared highly structured curriculum in basic studies. When new staff members are appointed, it is made clear at interviews that a desire both to work in a team and continually to prepare and revise teaching materials as resources are essential requirements for the job. The preparation of a tangible and transportable curriculum in language, reading, number and basic concepts has been conducted with the intention that the materials can be used in the home. The first community project established was a home-visiting scheme based on the Portage project in the USA. The educational psychologist attached to the school had seen a similar scheme in operation in another local authority, and had suggested the school develop a comparable project using their own materials. The original Portage project divides child development into a number of separate aspects and identifies a developmental sequence in each area. Children with special educational needs can have their profile of development pinpointed by matching their skills and behaviour against a checklist which divides development into *infant stimulation*, *socialization*, *language*, *self-help*, *cognitive* and *motor areas*. The headteacher and the educational psychologist were quick to envisage the benefit of a home-visiting scheme, as an aid to their work. For the psychologist it increased his 'referral options' and enabled him to help more children in perhaps the most effective place. He was also, on a number of occasions, able to make fundamental changes at comparatively little cost. The headteacher was keen on the preventive aspects of the scheme as well as the scope it afforded to concentrate solely on the development of the children.

The teachers work with parents in order to identify and specify what is required to assist the child to progress along the developmental sequence. The areas considered particularly important for physically handicapped children include language, sensory, independence or self-help skills – delayed or problematic, i.e. dressing, toileting, feeding. The special resource centre teacher, speech therapist, health visitor and a social worker are involved directly with the home. The teacher and parent draw up an activity chart which specifies a child's weekly learning programme, identifies the materials to be used for teaching the task, and the amount of time to be allotted to the learning of the task. The teacher assesses weekly progress and then negotiates new objectives. In general terms the scheme has begun as an encouraging success and has greatly assisted a large number of pupils with early learning difficulties as well as the physically handicapped pupils with associated developmental problems. Referrals for consideration for school placement, which are sent initially to the educational psychologist, come from a variety of sources – health visitors, social workers, GPs and parents themselves. Perhaps the most striking feature of the school is the level of staff involvement and commitment to the school's aims, and the difference the scheme makes to the pupils and parents involved.

Group learning situations

The challenge for the future in education, imposed by integration, is to decide the extent and kind of classroom grouping that best serve special needs and the teaching skills such grouping demands. McCall (1983) identifies the factors for consideration as the choice of characteristics which can be accurately assessed, which have a major influence on educational progress, which are stable, and enduring if the group arrangement they determine is to be a long-term affair, and which are acceptable to parents, teachers and the broader society. Grouping by specialist abilities and needs can determine more readily curricular needs meaningful to classroom social contexts. Where special curricula, special teaching methods, or both, are required by the placement of pupils with special needs in mainstream schools, the basic organization of the host school assumes critical importance. Meeting special needs calls for continuity of teaching and learning in an environment where teachers are able to fully utilize the experience of the pupil in establishing and maintaining a high degree of pupil involvement and motivation. To achieve these necessary conditions, a continuity of pupil – teacher contact and interaction is required, in order that the teacher or group leader has total control over the learning situation and can develop methods and approaches which bring to it the highest possible degree of flexibility and sensitivity. In the primary school the normal class or group teaching arrangements create something approaching these circumstances for all pupils, and hence it might be argued that the problem of meeting special needs within the normal organization are minimal.

Group activities

The purpose of group activity ought to be widely interpreted in order to identify the whole range of relationships with which a child has to learn to cope. Placement, in the classroom sense, can mean placement into a group for attainment level, language needs, social or emotional needs. Children requiring special educational provision may not have the latter needs well met if they remain for long periods of time in groups set up primarily on the basis of their level of attainment. An appropriate learning environment is fundamentally essential if special educational needs are to be fully met. Group activity embraces opportunities for leadership, subjectivity to the leadership of others, equal standing, co-operation, competition, conflict, confusion, and the give-and-take of peer relationships (McCall, 1983). The teacher responsible for initiating and guiding group activity, so excellently described by McCall, is:

(a) familiar with a range of group learning situations;
(b) able to classify group work by its purpose, and assess the needs of individual children in respect of the type of group learning they require;
(c) prepared to foster a flexible classroom environment in which many types of grouping occur over a term or year;
(d) aware of the effects of the *hidden curriculum* as transmitted by the total school environment.

But, though the arrangement approaches normality, does it always achieve it? It is clear that the mere presence of a handicapped child in a mainstream school does not, in itself, convert integration into interaction. Provision for the Sample Group of children with special needs in the survey schools shows a range of different organizations and some variety in standards achieved. Schools *B*, *H* and *I* attempt alternative provision, retaining the special school, given that a special school and mainstream schools are closely associated in a campus situation. Each school operates with its own headteacher and staff, but joint planning and organization have ensured the achievement of a good degree of interaction for pupils and staff, which will meet the needs of physically handicapped children, and offset the limitations of the special school. In theory, this arrangement should provide the 'best of both worlds' for children with special needs, through interaction which also extends the experience of the mainstream school pupils and staff, in a desirable manner. In practice, such an arrangement makes great demands on the staffs of both schools, and requires a high degree of co-operation, planning and supervision. Success appears to be well achieved at primary school level, where the organization of the mainstream and of the special school has most similarity. The physical surroundings of a properly planned 'campus' promotes movement and interaction. Headteachers and staffs must be efficiently briefed and motivated, and there must be interchange of staff as well as pupils to achieve proper maturity with the integration programme. The site requirements are critical, particularly in overcrowded urban areas.

Pupil interaction

The findings of the practical investigation revealed that headteachers of schools *B*, *H* and *I* had been briefed to co-operate with the adjoining special schools to secure the maximum interaction between handicapped and non-handicapped pupils. Site layouts were suited to the objective of interaction, given that the distances between the school buildings were reasonable, and excellent access to the buildings was available. The schools were well staffed by the standards of the local education authorities, and the quality of the staff was good, although school *B* had a high staff turnover. No additional staff had been allocated to the schools to foster interaction between the physically handicapped and able-bodied pupils, nor with the high ratio of socially disadvantaged pupils, and pupils of multi-ethnic origin. The standard of educational provision was high in each school, and the main interaction involved the brighter, more able physically handicapped child whom it was thought would gain from the stimulation provided in an environment with non-handicapped pupils of good intellectual potential. Opportunities were available for all physically handicapped pupils for group integrated activities and social interaction, in both the mainstream and special schools. Though satisfactory, and indicative of excellent prospects for this type of organized integration, improvement and greater development could be expected if, for example in school *B*, staffing ratios were increased and more ancillary help was made available. For fuller integration in schools *H* and *I*, much greater interaction between the staffs of both mainstream and special schools is necessary. It is essential that the issue of integration is made clear to the teachers involved, and written in the job description for headteachers, and that additional staffing allowances are made available to the campus in general, for the purpose of promoting integration.

Peer-tutoring

The group learning situation in school *I* revolved around working in pairs, which requires the participants to be relatively well-known to each other. It is important that one is not too dominant towards the other − many handicapped children are excessively dominant, that the level of ability, skill attainment relevant to the task in hand is of near equal standing in both parties or, if one pupil well exceeds the other in a specific developmental level, the former possesses empathy with the latter. This type of situation is valuable experience, and encourages peer communication, which can successfully lead to peer-tutoring amongst pupils with differing ability levels. Peer-tutoring[1] in school *I* has proved to be

---

[1]'Peer-tutoring means enlisting other children in the school to help those who are experiencing difficulties' (Reay, 1979).

a successful form of social collaboration between children with and without special needs. Reay (1979) comments generally on the approach and its value in enhancing self-esteem. In particular, time spent in applying themes and techniques from the various reading development activities, to children with special needs, has proved successful, not only for the enhancement of reading skill, but in applying variable grouping arrangements in the development of fundamental skills.

Most children with special needs require direct help in extending social awareness, finding better methods of managing peer relationships and an extended period of sensitivity training regarding 'taking the role of the other'. Small group arrangements were so designed, in schools *F*, *G* and *H*, to aid personal development and promote better behaviour planning as part of curricular activity, and Canfield and Wells (1976) similarly describe this successful application of role-playing group activity in a variety of group settings. Schools *B*, *C*, *E* and *I* organized opportunities for their pupils to come together in small groups for collective contribution to a resource outcome, for interchange of ideas prior to, or following, investigation by reading, watching, participating or listening, and to learn from the individual contributions of each group member. Small group formats are essential components of the educational provision for pupils with special needs, in particular children exhibiting learning difficulties, and demand a sense of belonging, a sense of co-operative effort, and the sharing of ideas and experience, as essential ingredients. The survey schools' successful work took account of the varied oral skills of group members, gave time for carefully explaining, regularly reviewing, and constantly monitoring, group projects, and provided different experiences for different personalities, which frequently arose from genuine motivated challenges, and encouraged further information 'research'. Work from one group is often used as a direct resource for another, and by such means children are encouraged to contribute directly to classroom resources. Also essential is an established atmosphere which encourages genuine *pupil assessment*, self-monitoring of work by individuals or groups, and provides the teacher with 'diagnostic' information regarding resources, which allows him to set a group the challenge of altering a resource to make it less difficult, more readily available, and more attractive.

Classroom groupings

Consideration was given in schools *A*, *D*, *G* and *H* to the different kinds of groupings for differing purposes within the classroom structure. Here, the teacher actively organizes different types of learning opportunity. He may encourage small group work, acting as a 'consultant' to such groups, and encouraging pupils to map out their own work, adapt to each other's pace, and discuss issues between themselves. The groups, including special needs pupils, may be of varied ability or homogeneous ability, or assembled around friendship ties or particular aspects of interest or 'research'. Together, such groups promote an exciting classroom atmosphere and offer greater possibility that all children profit from the created learning, which does not depend entirely on the teacher's output. These styles of teaching can be used easily and efficiently, if the teacher possesses a variety of resources drawn from commercial and traditional sources, which can be adapted effectively for use with pupils with special needs. Such adapted resources are initiated if teachers think flexibly about how key concepts or ideas are acquired by children and seek to present their teaching points by a variety of means of adaptation. Such varied classroom opportunities create many different social and intellectual opportunities, but any difficulty of monitoring what is happening and what is being achieved is surmountable, if assessment procedures are closely related to the type of learning activity taking place.

The purposes for which group work is designed take into account the fact that every teacher and every teacher-devised learning programme is individual in kind. Some of the major requirements of children with special educational needs, and the place of types of grouping, which, in part meet those needs, have been examined here. McCall (1983) emphasizes, 'It is important to realize these situations are more influential than merely being forms of social interaction or differing levels of adult/child autocracy.' Their presence allows for varied language experience, peer-tutoring, pupil initiation in the learning environment, and varied demands in respect of listening skill. Their absence means all of these developmental influences are likely to be non-existent or very restricted, and in terms of special educational provision, these facts are critical.

Classroom organization

Some children exhibiting special needs may need to spend part of their time in a daily group, the purpose of which is to encourage, via the use of discriminatory memory, description and summary tasks, greater attention skills. By careful developmental structuring, this acquiring of skills enables broader and more normal routine classroom assignments of mainstream work, as was seen in schools *C* and *F*. Schools *C*, *E* and *I* demonstrated an increase in the use of certain audiovisual means, programmed learning materials and structured kit materials, which extended the range of possible group work and as Hewett (1976) reminds us, this allows the teacher more time to concentrate on motivating, and rewarding group and individual attention skills attained. Halliday (1973) has outlined several functions of language, and it is debatable how far children can experience the full range of these functions without varied language opportunity in different group settings. Research by Tough (1976) found that teachers working with pupils with special educational needs require to be familiar with materials and methods that permit different communicative experiences in order to enhance the child's opportunity to experience the full range of language functions. There was found to be clear evidence of this in schools *B*, *C*, *D*, *H* and *I*, who were meeting the special educational needs of physically handicapped children from multicultural backgrounds.

Special resource class

The special resource class at school *E* was established in premises with suitable and total access for all physically handicapped children, and sited within the middle of the school building, so as to be fully integrated into the general life of the school. The amenities provided included a spacious teaching area, able to accommodate a maximum of 18 pupils, with a small room adjacent for individual work with pupils, a large activities room, which is used by the physiotherapist and speech therapist on a sessional basis, and an excellently equipped room adjoining, housing toileting and changing facilities, and used for school medicals and case conferences. Electric typewriters, possums and other specialist equipment have been provided as well as a wide range of educational materials required to meet the special educational needs of the pupils in the resource class. Capitation is provided through the school's main allocation, supplemented by the special education per capita allowance. A well qualified and experienced teacher has responsibility for the class, with the help of two ancillary staff – one full-time in the classroom situation, and the other working primarily as a physiotherapist's aid. The teacher-in-charge receives a special schools' allowance, but not a responsibility post, and this aspect is being currently investigated by the LEA. The ancillaries' primary responsibilities are to meet the physical needs of the children in the special resource class, to work generally as classroom aids and resource material providers, and also to carry out programmes designed by the speech therapists and physiotherapists.

From the outset, the intention was that the special resource class, was not to be run on 'unit' lines, i.e. pupils with disabilities were not to be grouped together and taught in a 'unit', with 'unit' staff accepting ultimate responsibility for the educational programmes of 'designated' children. The concept of the resource approach emerged, as the project got under way, thus giving it an educational philosophy framework for functioning, with a specific emphasis on adaptability and flexibility, aimed at meeting children's special needs in a mainstream school.

Flexible classroom arrangements

There are a number of considerations to be explored in relation to the flexible classroom arrangements, in evidence in six of the survey schools. Argyle (1972) differentiates between 'dominance' and 'dominant relationships' and suggests the effective teacher can exercise more efficient control through a dominant relationship, than by adopting the dominant role. Realistically, the dominant relationship implies many different relationships emanating from whole-class and part-class contact. If the teacher strives to offer children different forms of interaction, by performing leadership functions, giving feedback, contributing resources and suggesting courses of action, he will ultimately attain a good 'dominant relationship' with his class. However, such a state of affairs is only reached by conscious, consistent effort and the careful introduction of purposeful group arrangements. Docking (1980) reflects on the necessity of flexible social and learning opportunity, difficult to achieve in a well balanced way:

> It is perhaps a paradox that, in order to prepare the ground for developing relationships where status is given to pupil initiative, the teacher has first to 'define the situation' in terms of his own dominance. In doing this the teacher will be meeting the pupils' expectations that a teacher should be able to control them; at the same time the 'dominance' must be one which takes justice and caring seriously – for this too is what the pupils expect. Moreover, it is only a starting point to enable the teacher to educate the children to understand how they ought to regard relationships between persons.

When a physically handicapped child is placed in a mainstream class, careful consideration must be given to the selection of an appropriate environment, and priority to the inclusion of that pupil into the class group. One asset the non-handicapped child has, is the freedom of movement to allow him to see all of the classroom from different perspectives and to change perspectives at will. Movement is even more important for the physically handicapped child, given that it encourages and facilitates much incidental learning, and makes him feel he is part of his environment. Furniture must be arranged to facilitate free and easy movement, and activities should be planned to provide a vantage point to all areas of the room at some time during the day. This is essential for the physically handicapped child, who must avoid long periods of immobility to maintain and improve the level of motor function. The design of furniture for the child must afford flexibility for wheelchair users, and those pupils with standing aids and walking frames, and be sturdily built and durable. It is essential for orthopaedic development that desks and chairs are adjustable to the proper height for the individual child, and secured to take the weight of a disabled child, who might lean or fall.

All survey schools provided 'quiet areas' within the classroom, or small recesses adjoining the classroom area to be used by pupils, and particularly those with special needs, for small group activities or individual study. The cerebral palsied pupil, for example, who has uncontrolled or uncoordinated movements, works best from a quiet relaxed position. A great deal of noise and business prevents optimal learning conditions, especially for those pupils with a poor span of concentration, atypical of the spina bifida child. The physically handicapped child has less available energy than his non-handicapped peers, and often must make excessive demand on certain muscles to perform necessary tasks. For this reason, all adaptive methods and assistive devices are important to promote increased independence, educational progress and resultant self-esteem. The fieldwork in this investigation revealed many examples of practical arrangements which had been worked out and developed, to accommodate the needs of the handicapped pupil as well as those of the teacher and other pupils. Hardy and Cull (1974) point out that a stable environment provides a feeling of security and enhances the probability of successful learning and development, and where a pupil is comfortably positioned in an accessible environment, learning can become the prime focus of attention.

Teaching aids

Physically handicapped pupils with very little manual control in schools *B, C, E, F, G* and *I* have the use of electric typewriters. Possum typewriters are used in schools *C* and *E* for two pupils with no manual control; one controlled by feet, and the other by the head, with the use of a pointer attached to a strap around the child's head. Typewriter shields help those pupils with uncontrolled movements, and adjustable slant boards and tables enable the children to reach the keys with a minimum amount of effort. For pupils with eye–hand co-ordination difficulties, book holders and slant boards are used, and page turners, automatic and manual, were also in evidence. Communication boards, used by non-communicating pupils in schools *C, E* and *F* enabled the children to indicate appropriate responses on the board, and one pupil with the ability to point to the item or letter he wanted on a communication board used the direct selection method. Scanning, in its simplest form, is used by two pupils in school *F*, and presents words, pictures or verbal questions to a child, one at a time. The pupil indicates yes, when the correct message is received, by virtue of a smile, nod or other pre-arranged signal. A higher-level scanning device presents letters one at a time, and the pupil indicates the letters to spell his message. This approach is successfully used in schools *C* and *F*, with severely physically handicapped pupils, who have useful hand control, and those multipli-handicapped pupils whose cognitive capabilities limit them to responding only to spoken words or pictures of basic objects. Hence, the schools considered communication as the foundation of learning, and so established reliable communication systems for the physically handicapped pupils, with maximum support possible for the teacher, from ancillary assistants, speech therapists, and advisory and support teachers.

A well-planned, written curriculum is a major step towards public understanding of the functions of special educational provision, and all pupils, with and without special needs, should have access to four broad areas of the curriculum:

1. The basic skills of language and mathematics.
2. The study of people, their relationships and their achievements, both in current society and at other times and in other places.
3. A study of both biological and physical aspects of the environment and how people are affected by the environment and how, in turn, they use it.
4. Practical activity, imaginative experience and creative expression (Wilson, 1981).

Evaluations of the learning environment are experiences likely to directly affect learning, especially if the resultant success or failure is immediately acted upon. Evaluation is concerned with the effectiveness of the school as a community and it is a valuable exercise for the staff to review the school in this way from time to time. The curriculum will not be static if the evaluation is valid and effective – it will change and develop along with increased understanding, changing roles, and groups of pupils with differing special educational needs.

7
Social and Emotional Dimensions

Hegarty and Pocklington (1981) take the view that 'the development of young people with special needs and the relationships they form, are governed by many factors relating to the school and the individuals themselves'. The teacher's role, personality, teaching style and the implicit social messages transmitted by the teacher through individual teaching style, will directly or indirectly shape a child's social and emotional behaviour, and the social relationships he can or cannot tolerate. The way in which pupils are taught has important implications for independence and requires the formation of positive attitudes, on the part of all concerned. This approach must embrace staff at every level in the school and relevant attitudes must be embodied in appropriate procedures and practical arrangements within that school. Attitudes are influenced by the nature of the special needs, and the local situation, the factors of which require to be taken into account before the individual can apply them in the light of knowledge. However, the relevance of local factors is not confined to those with special needs, since the school ethos that promotes independence for a sub-group is likely to do so for the whole school.

Ethos of the school

It has been suggested that special provision in mainstream schools for small groups of handicapped pupils can sometimes result in social isolation and rejection by their non-handicapped peers. Yet, from the information received from parents, pupils and the schools themselves, the 50 severely handicapped children in this survey have generally found that placement in a mainstream school, coupled with emotional support given by various support staff in direct contact with them, has meant the creation of a social environment which offers as much support as they individually need. Such an environment offers wider opportunities for meaningful social relationships with both non-handicapped and handicapped fellow pupils.

The survey indicated that where physically handicapped pupils were being placed in the new situation of a mainstream school, the teachers who would work directly with them were somewhat anxious as to how well they would be accepted by their peers. In some cases, there was scope for the social environment to be modified in a variety of ways, and generally the non-handicapped pupils were given some advance information about the handicapped pupils, about their special needs, and given suggestions as to the type of behaviour towards them which would be appropriate. Several pupils in the survey had a gross disfigurement caused by the handicap, yet there was no element of repulsion evident within the peer group. All the pupils in the sample group had a handicap which was recognizable, yet all were readily accepted by their non-handicapped peers. There was general agreement amongst the headteachers of the survey schools and their staffs that there were no major social problems. To the contrary, there were several instances of pupils from emotionally disturbed and socially deprived backgrounds forming positive and meaningful friendships with pupils with special physical needs, hence avoiding the possibility of they themselves becoming isolates. Such relationships therefore are of two-way benefit, and promote a social dimension which is worthy of development.

The influence of emotional and behavioural problems

Schools *C*, *E* and *I* suggested physically handicapped pupils who had difficulties coping with the mainstream of the school's teaching had significantly less friends. Staff, however, identified two key factors in the improvement in pupils' behaviour and socialization techniques: having normal behaviour models to copy, and being subject to firm discipline. Many teachers commented on the importance of physically handicapped pupils being exposed to other behaviour patterns, besides those of fellow handicapped peers. Being surrounded by normality can make a big difference to their behavioural patterns. As mentioned earlier, groups of pupils from the campus special school adjacent to schools *H* and *I* exhibited odd and grossly immature behaviour when participating in group integrated activities in the mainstream school, yet, when integrated individually for specific activities in the mainstream school, this did not happen other than by way of exception. Mainstream school staff commented on the somewhat abnormal atmosphere in the special school. A pertinent example which illustrates the general point serves as a reminder that imitation can be a two-way process. The behaviour of one girl who spent a period of time in a special school following major corrective orthopaedic surgery was considered by staff at the mainstream school to have deteriorated, when she returned there. This was attributed to too much attention being given her, which resulted in lack of independence and an apathetic attitude, and loss of interest in school work. The result was poor presentation of work of an inferior quality, because of a low level of ability and hence a lack of appropriate stimulus, amongst members of the class group in which she was placed.

But, pupils did not always copy their peers. There was some evidence that they responded directly to ridicule or rebuke when their behaviour or appearance made them stand out. As they grew in self-awareness and formed or sought to form relationships with other pupils, they strove to conform to peer group expectations. This led to considerable modification of behaviour. Teachers' positive expectations of their pupils had a normalizing effect, and there was a broad consensus of opinion among teachers and parents, that the pupils had benefited in terms of social and emotional development.

Emotional or behavioural problems clearly influence personal relationships and there are many ways in which a physical handicap may affect emotional development. It is often assumed that physically handicapped pupils will show more emotional disturbance than their peers, because they are likely to be frequently frustrated. Teachers in the mainstream classes with physically handicapped members listed the frustrations which a handicapped pupil was likely to experience, and observed the different ways of coping, and how successful they were. From these observations, the teachers were able to understand and become more aware of the reasons for certain frustrations. It was generally agreed that they were imposed not always by the handicap, but frequently by the environment, and the staff of the survey schools felt unanimously that once such frustrations and their causes had been identified, compromises could usually be reached, either to combat them or to avoid them. Close liaison with parents was considered to be of extreme value in identifying the background to the frustrations.

Motivation towards independence

The achievement of independence is a complex process and many psychological variables have a bearing on it. Motivation however is the crucial factor in achieving independence – an assessment by 80 per cent of the teaching staff in the Sample Group. Their aim was to highly motivate their pupils to achieve, both for the school and for themselves, so that they would reach a level of independence and maturity which aided social acceptance. An important consideration in the development of independence is the role played by a policy of encouraging it, which helps pupils to be independent. Hegarty and Pocklington (1982) describe clear prescriptions for action, to enable teachers to promote independence, relating to formal teaching geared explicitly to independence, the teaching of other subjects so as to promote independence, and the maintaining of an atmosphere of autonomy. Children are more likely to behave in an independent manner if that is what is expected of them. This is related to findings of the *Barker Lunn Children's Attitude Scales*, on the relationship between expectation and academic achievement. Relevance to pupils with special needs is particularly illustrated by those who suffer from low expectations. There was evidence in three survey schools of a reversal of these expectations giving pupils faith in themselves and leading to their becoming far more independent. Higher expectations were attributed, by the staff, to giving specific responsibilities to pupils with special needs, making a minimum of interventions and allowing for necessary concessions only, and discouraging immature behaviour.

The development of independence is a major target, and within the process of integration there is a correlation between independence and social acceptance. A large number of parents of handicapped pupils commented on the measurable growth in independence, in recognition of their child's social acceptance as a member of the mainstream school. It is of relevant interest to note that the staff of the two mainstream campus schools commented on how the groups of special school pupils integrated for group activities, and, individually, for selected activities, on a regular basis, were totally dependent on the special school, and remained at a relatively immature level. Various factors influence the degree of independence achieved: level of supervision and staff support; opportunities for independent action and decision making; psychological factors, especially motivation, and a policy of encouraging independence. Some staff argued that too high a level of supervision and support were detrimental and prevented pupils from growing in independence. Others felt they lacked the knowledge and expertise that would sensitize them to particular needs. Six members of staff in school *E* felt strongly that independence is not an absolute goal, and by pursuing it as blanket policy pupils' individual needs may not be met. In school *C*, the staff had a clearly identifiable philosophy, and advocated reduced supervision and support for positive reasons. One teacher commented that 'education is for life, and is not a sheltered workshop'.

The impression gained from the staff of schools *B* and *I* was that the insistence on independent action from pupils, led pupils to believe in themselves and so become more independent. The 18 pupils with experience of special as well as mainstream schools were quite sure that in the mainstream school they were 'more like other children' and could do more things for themselves. None wanted to return to a special school, and one seven-year-old said 'You are not handicapped at this school!' The mainstream school was considered by another handicapped pupil to offer 'the chance of being a person who doesn't have to depend on people to do things for you'.

In mainstream schools, pupils with special needs are likely to have opportunities for independent action and decision making, because the staff are concerned for all pupils and cannot devote too much time to the few with special needs, even if they wish to do so. The two survey schools with special resource classes felt good staffing ratios created the necessary conditions for independent action. As an example, dressing, toileting, changing calipers, can all take a good deal of time if pupils do the tasks themselves. The staffing ratio must adequately allow for staff to repeatedly show them how, and to be available when needed, in a supportive role for as long as is necessary for full independence to be achieved. Another school, where staffing ratios were poor, admitted that they attended to the pupils' physical needs themselves, in order to save a great deal of time, yet staff were fully aware that they were depriving them of a most important opportunity for developing personal independence.

Factors influencing social relationships

In an earlier study of integration in primary schools, Anderson (1973) suggests:

> While disability may influence a social relationship in a very direct way by placing limits on motorbility and on the range of activities which may be important in sustaining the relationship, less obvious factors are often operating... A child who is threatened by competence in physical skills or who is not fully accepted by his peers may feel handicapped children to be less threatening and less competent and more likely to accept him.

This would seem a perfectly logical explanation for the behaviour of the small number of socially 'at risk' pupils who developed friendships with their physically handicapped peers. However, some disappointment was indicated concerning eight physically handicapped pupils, fully integrated in mainstream schools, who were not interacting with their non-handicapped peers as well as had been hoped. In the main, these pupils had communication difficulties, were of low ability level and exhibited severe learning difficulties. It was felt because of these factors, these pupils found difficulty in coping with the odd incidents of teasing, the answering of questions about their handicap, and in some respects, lacked the social confidence to develop a positive self-image. These pupils initially sought the attention of staff, and sometimes spent break and lunchtime periods alone. A relevant and similar observation was made by both teaching and ancillary staff, in relation to other pupils with special needs who were considered 'at risk' socially and emotionally. The staff of school *H* unanimously agreed that such pupils could present much greater problems than those with physical handicaps, and felt social interaction between the two parties was a helpful and positive contribution to school life.

Promotion of self-confidence

Social integration, mixing with their age peers and forming relationships outside the 'handicapped' community is important both in its own right and as a factor in promoting self-confidence and maturity amongst pupils with special needs. The impression gained, based on interviews with school staff, pupils and parents, plus personal observation, is that there are grounds for guarded optimism; normal relationships are possible, and negative ones can be avoided. There is specific evidence that the nature of relationships and good friendships between pupils with special needs and their non-handicapped peers depend on many factors. For instance, friendly relationships at first school age tended to fluctuate frequently, as is the norm, and formed no specific pattern. At middle school age, such relationships tended to be consistent with peers of similar personality, and those with common interests and, in general, friendships were more constant. Relationships were at their easiest and most natural when handicapped pupils were integrated on an individual basis. Reasons were identified why pupils with special needs should form relationships with their similar peers, rather than other pupils. For example, their friendships tended to be with those closest to hand, and hence for many pupils with special needs in the mainstream school, these will be other pupils with special needs. 'They', suggested one teacher, 'have common experiences, and a closer understanding of each other's special conditions and needs'. Pupils stayed within their own group at the beginning, but gradually built up relationships within the class group, in schools *C* and *E*, where large groups of physically handicapped pupils were integrated.

Handicapped pupils individually integrated, or integrated in situations where they did not stand out as a separate group, were most likely to form relationships in which the special need was irrelevant. Some relationships were determined primarily by personality and other individual characteristics just as they are for any other pupil. School *C* commented that when the integration programme first started, the physically handicapped pupils were entering a situation where the main body of pupils were well known to each other. There were pre-existing patterns of relationships and there could have been considerable peer pressure against association with them. This was, however, considered a situation similar to other outgroups, and hence not a problem related specifically to handicap, so much as to the more general one of combining disparate groups into a special and functional whole. In school *F*, the primary contacts the physically handicapped pupils had were with each other, and with those who were themselves perhaps members of the school's outgroup; the immature and socially unsuccessful, the underachieving, and occasionally, the disruptive. However, the school reported a number of examples of close and enduring friendships developing. Relationships were more likely to occur when older pupils, especially girls, befriended younger pupils and mothered them. When a physically handicapped boy first came to infant school, his teacher described how there was competition to wheel him around the playground. There were numerous examples of young physically handicapped pupils 'at risk' of being adopted in this way, but whilst the tendency was most pronounced on the occasion of pupils' first arrival at school, it commonly diminished with familiarity, and the passage of time.

There was evidence in schools *A*, *D* and *G* of pupils seeking to befriend those with special needs, or assist them in practical ways, often from a sense of duty. Staff suggested this might be the result of moral or religious convictions, or a response to exhortations by staff, but felt they were mostly relationships of helping rather than of equal friendship. In a few cases this process did lead, with the increase of familiarity and respect, to relationships of equality but, equally, there was firm evidence of the prevailing attitude, after a lengthy period of time, still being one of kindness to the handicapped. The occurrence of negative relationships can produce anxiety amongst parents of physically handicapped pupils, and others fearing pupils with special needs are at risk in the 'rough and tumble' of the mainstream school. Many shy and sensitive youngsters can find the social milieu of some schools extremely trying, but Hegarty and Pocklington (1982) remind us, 'pupils with special needs do not in general benefit from being seen in need of protection; they benefit, rather, from the assumption that they are as psychologically robust as other pupils, and being immersed in the rough and tumble of school life'. Negative incidents and patterns of relationships identified in the practical investigation were comparatively rare, and those that did occur were not regarded as major problems.

Although likelihood of contact between pupils with special needs and their peers depends on many interconnected factors, the most important aspect is the pupil's own personality. Whether a pupil was popular or unpopular, had many friends or few, was teased or not, depended very much on personality factors. Many pupils with severe handicapping conditions were popular in spite of them, because of their warmth and good humour, while others were unpopular because of sullenness or tiresome behaviour, just as happens with all pupils. There was evidence of handicap considerations receding in favour of personality factors, as relationships developed. A second factor to consider is ability level, and physically handicapped pupils who are academically able seem to enjoy normal relationships with their able-bodied peers. By contrast, those who have learning difficulties in addition, are less fortunate, and their social contact tends to be with similar peers or with slow learners. Relationships at first school level are relatively fluid and perhaps less determined by personality characteristics. Children of that age have a degree of spontaneous interest in most things around them, and in particular the various aids and gadgets used by the physically handicapped pupil. One teacher from school *F* described how the physically handicapped child was persuaded to 'give up' his wheelchair at lunchtimes, so that his non-handicapped peers could have rides around the playground! School *E* said electric typewriters were a big attraction, and it was much more novel to play ball games with walking aids rather than feet.

Undesirable behaviour

Physically handicapped pupils may exhibit behaviour that is socially undesirable, but not disruptive or unacceptable. The practical investigation produced examples of grossly immature behaviour, odd mannerisms and poor eating habits. In general, as far as physically handicapped pupils with associated learning difficulties were concerned, the main constraints on integration seemed to be behavioural ones. There was some evidence of pupils deliberately using their handicaps in a mischievous way. School *I* cited an example of a senior pupil propelling her wheelchair into a group of children, virtually pushing them out of the way, and often causing sharp blows to their legs. Another child in school *C* was in the habit of strategically placing her crutch to cause other pupils to trip. However, the victims did retaliate, and the wheelchair child sometimes found herself pushed with some force, along the corridor, and left to her own devices to bring herself to a halt. The child walking with crutches found herself occasionally jostled and overbalanced. Hence, although turning unfavourable incidents into assets in this way did little good for relationships, at least it allowed the children to learn the rudiments of 'fair play'!

There was general agreement amongst the staff in the Sample Group regarding the importance of punishment for pupils with special needs, at the same level as for all pupils; the same rules and regulations must apply. If non-handicapped peers are urged to accept pupils with special needs as equals, then if the latter group infringe pupil codes of behaviour, or trade on their handicap status, they must not be accorded a privileged position. Retaliation, as described above, in moderation, constitutes an important lesson for learning. Several teachers drew attention to the fact that pupils with special needs could be aggravating or antisocial because of personality factors. The child in school *I* who badly frightened children with her wheelchair was most unpopular because of her domineering and sarcastic attitude. Schools *E* and *F* made a few references to pupils' grossly immature patterns of behaviour – temper tantrums, crying outbursts, throwing of books, pencils, etc. to the floor, when frustrated or unable to have their own way. Encouragingly, however, staff reported less aggression, less odd attention-seeking behaviour, better table manners and so on, given time, than when the pupils first came to the school.

Anxiety

When individual items of behaviour, seen amongst the handicapped pupils, were considered, the two major problems identified were worrying, resulting in some anxiety, and fearfulness, indicating a certain lack of confidence. Avoiding the situation seemed to be considered the easiest way out of a problem by a small percentage of pupils (16 per cent) and five pupils were very resentful of correction. Although it is generally accepted that the presence of a handicap may give rise to frustration and uncertainty, the fact that different handicapped children react in entirely different ways to frustrative and uncertain situations is thought to be determined by the individual parental attitude to handicap. Brennan (1982a) suggests: 'The child seems to adopt the same attitude to disability as his parents do', and the likelihood that he will develop related emotional disorders reflects the attitudes of acceptance or rejection. Relationships are a two-way process and are affected by characteristics of the main pupil body as well, of which two of the most important are the related factors of familiarity and understanding. Association between pupils with special needs and their peers is not only a problem for the former. Non-handicapped pupils can have difficulty in knowing how to react, and this can lead to avoidance behaviour and other negative responses. But these are natural reactions, and no more prevalent in schools than in society at large. The lack of understanding can lead to rejection and uncertainty, and timidness can result in stilted relationships or the total avoidance of contact. Evidence showed that where teachers in the survey schools had prepared, however simply, their pupils for the integration of pupils with special needs, initial natural reactions could be, and often were, replaced by more positive attitudes.

Opportunities for social interaction

Within the school day

There are many opportunities for legitimate social contact during lessons, quite apart from the social activities that pupils set up independently of the teacher. Excellent examples were to be seen in schools *A*, *C*, *E* and *I* of pupils, handicapped and non-handicapped, working on group projects where each had an assigned role, and structured interaction was essential. Discussions can involve the whole class, experimental work may necessitate working together or sharing equipment; craft and practical work affords opportunities for casual chatter. Frequently to be seen in all the survey schools were pupils with special needs working side by side with other pupils and included in conversations both naturally and spontaneously. There was a general feeling amongst staff, however, that preparation is necessary to ensure that pupils are not isolated in the classroom and that opportunities for contact with non-handicapped peers are fostered. Staff in school *F* suggested that the presence of more than one pupil with special needs in the class can result in less interaction with able-bodied friends. A teacher from school *G* emphasized that 'it is of extreme importance to encourage the physically handicapped pupil that he also has to give in order to take of other pupils' experiences'. Another member of staff from school *C* felt that pupils with special needs must learn what is acceptable, and what is not acceptable behaviour, when with their peers. The presence of ancillaries or support/specialist teachers might hinder easy spontaneous contact in the classroom, particularly if they are concerned exclusively with the pupil with special needs. With the exception of survey schools *B*, *F* and *G*, the teaching staffs and some physically handicapped pupils preferred to be without ancillary support, on a full-time basis in the classroom environment. There was evidence in seven of the nine schools of ancillaries seeking to minimize the interference, by adopting a more general role in the classroom, and helping with all pupils as requested by the teacher.

Official breaktimes are essentially the most important for social interaction, when pupils are freed from lessons and for the most part from adult supervision. They interact socially in various ways in accordance with their age, facilities available and so forth. As far as pupils with special needs are concerned, their participation will be governed by the nature of their handicapping conditions, the physical environment of the school, and practical factors such as whether the special resource class has its break at the same time as the rest of the school. Interaction occurs more spontaneously amongst younger children, who are less sensitive to differences, and do not appear to notice handicapping conditions as much as older pupils. Also, the disparity in development increases with age in some cases. The nature of the social interaction between pupils is different at different ages, in ways which affect integration possibilities. At infant level, play is loosely structured and dependent on spontaneity; it can begin and end, and change direction at any time, and often has a high non-verbal component. Such a basis enables pupils with special needs to participate more easily. The aim, however, must be to use arrangements to promote interaction in such a way that more general relationships develop, and pupils are therefore presented with the opportunity of mixing with their peers. Lunchtime is another occasion for possible social interaction. Teachers gave two specific responses to this situation. Some considered special needs pupils were better off on their own, and therefore made separate arrangements for them, whilst others believed they must learn to cope with the hurly burly of large crowds, and hence arranged for them to eat with their peers, with and without adult support. Mealtimes are important learning occasions for some pupils – structured feeding programmes can be implemented, table manners taught and so on. Some teachers judged the learning opportunities, and the close personal contact which certain opportunities demanded, as being more important than any social benefits to be gained from integration.

Whether or not integration takes place depends on a considerable number of factors, many of them at the discretion of the school. Gottlieb *et al* (1974) suggest that merely placing the non-handicapped and handicapped together may not, of itself, increase the latter's willingness to accept the former socially. The handicapped can avoid contact with other children, and so other children do not necessarily interact with them. Guralnick (1978) emphasized that 'play behaviour is a key ingredient in adaptability learning, cognition, education and social behaviour'. The involvement of peers, as *peer tutors*, which has become increasingly evident in the USA and Canada during the last few years, was evident in three of the survey schools. The advantages are described as the potential existing in peer interaction being utilized for constructive educational ends; the tutoring situation being beneficial to both partners; and the invaluable assistance provided for the teacher. In the other six schools, there was little emphasis placed on promoting interaction between pupils with special needs and their peers in a formal way.

Extra-curricular activities

Generally, the schools looked to the aspects of locational integration to be extended, and to lead on to a degree of social integration. The main purpose of lunchtime clubs and societies was to facilitate interaction between the two groups. In the two campus situations, special school staff organized activities for their pupils and pupils from the host school, and the pupils from the special school joined their non-handicapped peers in the host school for a variety of integrated activities. One school, *C*, 'twinned' each handicapped pupil with a non-handicapped pupil, initially, and hence a liaison was formed. However, as the handicapped pupils formed other friendships, the twinning process was allowed to fluctuate, usually towards the end of the first term.

During this period of time, observation of the peer interaction was carried out, to assess the impact of the intervention. The results were most encouraging and a significant increase in the amount of co-operative play and associative play was recorded between the two groups of handicapped and non-handicapped pupils. There were no instances of solitary play, being unoccupied or being an onlooker, and less incidence of the handicapped choosing their fellow handicapped pupils as their only friends. This success demonstrated how social interaction can be achieved by a change in attitude brought about by established and properly planned guidelines. There is a case to be made for adults to make more explicit intervention than is the norm in order to promote social interaction between pupils with special needs and their peers. The indirect steps which can be taken to remove obstacles and constraints must be explored, to ensure that the school's everyday organization does not contribute to the isolation of pupils with special needs.

It was noted in schools *C* and *F*, which had special resource classes, that the physically handicapped pupils were slightly more outgoing and confident. Perhaps such a class offered a more secure environment for pupils with special needs. However it was encouraging to observe from the teachers' stated opinions that only three physically handicapped pupils were considered to be significantly lacking in confidence in relation to their respective class groups, and generally teachers felt their physically handicapped pupils derived confidence from the sheer fact of being in a mainstream school. In the majority of cases, the pupils with special needs did not feel different from their peers and were not aware that they were different. Indeed, the practical investigation showed that even pupils with severe and complex needs can be educated in mainstream schools with a positive enhancement to their self-esteem. Six of the nine survey schools provided sufficient sub-group opportunities for pupils with special needs to gain a sense of achievement and develop their self-esteem. In school *I*, a senior spina bifida pupil had become an accomplished clarinet player with the school orchestra, while a partially-sighted spina bifida pupil was a successful chess player who had participated in inter-school tournaments. A number of physically handicapped pupils acted as school librarians, classroom monitors, members of school choirs, and regularly played major roles in school plays and concerts. Schools *B*, *C*, *E* and *I* organized annual school camps and hostel holidays, in which a large number of physically handicapped pupils participated, and several pupils had gained county awards in swimming. It may well be assumed that handicapped pupils are very keen to be included in the full range of school activities.

Transport restrictions

It is necessary to examine the opportunities available for social interaction, at different stages of the school day: before and after school; assembly; registration and form periods; classroom activities; break-times and lunch periods. When handicapped pupils attend mainstream schools, this presents an opportunity to rethink special transport policies. The distance criterion is no longer relevant in certain cases, as some pupils make their way to and from school independently as a direct result of an integration programme. It would seem that there are occasions when special transport is necessary, occasions when it is probably desirable and occasions when it is unnecessary and not in the pupil's best interests. When pupils are brought to school by special transport, there is not only no opportunity for contact with non-handicapped pupils on the way to and from school, but the distinctiveness of pupils with special needs is reinforced in a very public way. The isolation imposed by special transport can be compounded by further factors such as reception arrangements, length of school day, and constraints imposed by taxi schedules. In response to an item in their questionnaire, regarding transport, teachers commented as follows:

Teachers' questionnaires

Section A: 1. Transport	(i)	Mini-bus provided by LEA	15
		Taxi provided by LEA	17
		Car provided by LEA	6
		Car provided by parents	4
		Pushchair/walking	2
	(ii)	Escort + driver (LEA employed)	37
		Driver only	1
		Parent	4
		Elder sibling	2
	(iii)	Lateness due to traffic/weather	34
		Late delivery/early collection	13
		Unable to participate in extra-curricular activities	30
		No problems	6

It is interesting to note the diversity with regard to special transport policy, and that in only six instances did teachers feel the special transport arrangements currently in force presented no problems.

In some cases, pupils were dropped at the main school entrance, and taken straight inside the school by a waiting, conscientious ancillary. 'A little less conscientiousness', suggest Hegarty and Pocklington (1981), 'and the pupil could spend some time with peers before school began'. In four schools, pupils with special needs had a shorter school day than their peers because of transport schedules. It is not clear what educational justification there is for this anomaly, but as far as integration is concerned, it is an anachronism that needs to be disposed of promptly, because it totally precludes any possibility of contact, at the beginning and end of the school day. There were numerous instances of special transport arriving consistently late, as is shown in the above table.

This was greatly disruptive to teaching programmes, as was the fact that these same pupils who arrived late were expected to be ready for departure before the end of the official school day. Two schools were attempting to wean pupils from special transport both for the independence it promoted, and the social opportunities it created. Another factor which affected relationships was that many of the handicapped pupils lived outside the catchment area of the school, sometimes a considerable distance away. This meant that friendships could not be continued after school, and there was less opportunity to take part in extra-curricular activities, when relationships might have been cemented. Special transport imposed further restrictions, given that times of arriving and leaving school ones was strictly scheduled, and could not be changed or negotiated. Some teachers in the survey schools felt very strongly that more flexible arrangements for transporting special needs pupils were long overdue. Rarely were there problems when parents privately transported their children to and from school.

School assembly

School assembly is a feature of the British education system of extraordinary scope and diversity. The list is readily expanded so that assemblies have a multiplicity of functions. This makes them a prime vehicle for promoting integration in that it makes, or can be made to make, minimal demands on participants, and allows flexibility in that any pupil can be given a role to enact, however briefly, in front of the entire school. A fundamental reason for including pupils with special needs in assembly is that it is an activity of the whole school, and an expression, however imperfect, of the school's corporate identity. Attendance at assembly reinforces that everyone, pupil and teacher, has a share in that identity. With regard to social contact, this clearly depends on individual arrangements. There is, perhaps, little to be said for the purely locational integration that occurs in formal assemblies. Therefore, when special transport came late, pupils arrived during assembly, disrupted it, or missed it altogether. In some schools, however, assembly was held midmorning, immediately before break, and this arrangement seemed a sensible compromise.

Adjustment to handicap

A major aspect of maturity is adjustment to handicap, in the sense of becoming aware of the limitations associated with it, and gradually accepting them. The problems of adjustment, which children with special needs experience, are broadly of two kinds. They may become inward looking and attach too much importance to their handicapping condition, seeing themselves as special cases and deserving of sympathy and exceptional status. Others betray a lack of realism and failure to adjust to their handicap, by nurturing wildly ambitious dreams with little appreciation of what is entailed to realize them. Here, the role of the mainstream school is to provide a stimulating environment that promotes adjustment and immerses in 'normality', but some pupils with special needs become better adjusted, while others do not. There was clear evidence that the self-esteem of physically handicapped pupils could be significantly enhanced from placement in a mainstream school. The headteacher of school *E* took the view that being confined to a wheelchair did not mean the child could not cope with being in a class of able-bodied peers, because he might be upset by their freedom of movement. Several teachers expressed the opinion that many people become hypersensitive when confronted with handicap, and 'imagined' the experience of being handicapped, which could result in a tendency to underestimate the psychological aptitude of pupils with special needs.

Influential factors

Various factors influence the adjustment of pupils with special needs in an environment not geared specifically to them, and where allowances are not automatically made. It was apparent that seven of the nine schools had tackled this successfully by making a minimum of fuss and exception, which gave dramatic improvements in the pupils' projected self-image. The child's image of himself, particularly those aspects of the self-concept relating to attitudes, and experiences involving the body, are likely to be intensified when he is integrated with non-handicapped peers. In many respects the handicapped child will want to share the peer values, particularly as regards physical activity, hence the handicap may well become a latent source of self-devaluation. When a handicapped child first goes to school, he has then to face the responsibility for his own adjustment to the new school world. The school environment is a complex one, and if the handicap is not well accepted by the parents, it is at this point that an increase in emotional problems can be expected, which escalate even more so in adolescence. Where the handicap is well accepted, the handicapped child is confidently more realistic in his self descriptions, and is able to share the aspirations of his non-handicapped peers, whilst accepting he cannot live up to them.

From the data provided by the parents and school staffs, it would appear that the majority of handicapped pupils in the Sample Group were well-adjusted to their handicaps. In just four cases (eight per cent), were there obvious signs of emotional disturbance, due to difficulties in accepting the handicap, racial prejudice, and failure to adjust totally to mainstream school placement. Schools *B, C* and *I* stressed that by requiring their pupils with special needs to make adjustments continually, and providing a supportive environment within which they could do so, these pupils do not have to make such big adjustments when they transfer to secondary education, because there is a feeling of belonging to the mainstream school. There was a general feeling amongst the staffs of these schools that physically handicapped pupils need to be helped to realize that they have to try harder than their peers to reach the same targets, and placement in a mainstream school can teach them an invaluable lesson. In contrast, however, the staff of schools *E* and *F*, where non-selective programmes of integration for physically handicapped pupils were in operation, felt that emotional adjustment for pupils with special needs could be hindered when placed in a mainstream school, because of lack of specialist help, inadequate preparation, and because the opportunities presented are not always recognized by the staff concerned.

Gains in self-confidence and independence

There were gains in self-confidence and independence in evidence amongst physically handicapped pupils in all the survey schools, and it might be said that the integration of pupils with special needs in the mainstream school promoted a realistic acceptance of the individual handicapping condition. What is of substantial interest is the range of factors bearing on social and emotional development, which the practical investigation has illustrated. The general picture can be further illustrated by reference to the Barker Lunn findings, fully described in the following tables.

Barker Lunn Children's Attitude Scales: Results

For use with 9 – 11 year olds, i.e. 50 per cent of the Sample Group and their respective Control Groups, intended for research purposes to examine broad differences. Highest number indicates a most favourable score and lowest number a least favourable score.

A.	Score on 'attitude to school' scale	Physically handicapped		Above average ability		Below average ability	
Range of score	6	13	52%	12	48%	7	28%
	5	10	40%	8	32%	5	20%
	4	2	8%	5	20%	9	36%
	3					3	12%
	2					1	4%
	1						
	0						
	Number of pupils	25		25		25	
	Mean score	5.44		5.28		4.56	

Inference: Physically handicapped pupils have the most favourable attitude to school in respect of general, rather than specific, aspects of school life. All 25 physically handicapped and 25 above average ability pupils are considered to have a favourable attitude to school, compared with a favourable attitude amongst 21 below average ability pupils. Four below average ability pupils are considered to have a negative attitude.

B. Score on 'interest in school work' scale	Physically handicapped		Above average ability		Below average ability	
6	8	32%	10	40%	5	20%
5	16	64%	11	44%	12	48%
4	1	4%	4	16%	5	20%
3					0	0%
2					2	8%
1					1	4%
0						
Number of pupils	25		25		25	
Mean score	5.28		5.24		4.56	

Range of score applies to column 1.

Inference: The physically handicapped pupils show the most interest in school work, just slightly ahead of the above average ability pupils. Five below average ability pupils show less interest, and three others significantly less interest.

C. Score on 'importance of doing well' scale	Physically handicapped		Above average ability		Below average ability	
10	5	20%	9	36%	4	16%
9	8	32%	6	24%	4	16%
8	8	32%	8	32%	7	28%
7	3	12%	0	0%	2	8%
6	1	4%	2	8%	3	12%
5					1	4%
4					2	8%
3					1	4%
2					1	4%
1						
0						
Number of pupils	25		25		25	
Mean score	8.52		8.8		7.28	

Range of score applies to column 1.

Inference: This scale is made up of items stressing achievement-orientation. Above average ability pupils' scores show it is most important to do well in school, whilst a small number of the Sample and Control Groups consider it reasonably important. Four pupils of below average ability consider it unimportant.

D.	Score on 'attitude to class' scale	Physically handicapped		Above average ability		Below average ability	
Range of score	15–16	16	64%	14	56%	9	36%
	13–14	6	24%	8	32%	9	36%
	11–12	3	12%	2	8%	3	12%
	9–10			1	4%	2	8%
	7–8					1	4%
	5–6					1	4%
	3–4						
	1–2						
	0						
	Number of pupils	25		25		25	
	Mean score	15.04		14.8		13.6	

Inference: This scale refers to the favourableness or otherwise of being a member of a particular school class. The physically handicapped pupils and the above average ability Control Group scores suggest favourable attitudes to their class, whilst only two below average ability pupils appear to have a poor attitude.

E.	Score on 'other image of class' scale	Physically handicapped		Above average ability		Below average ability	
Range of score	6	18	72%	12	48%	6	24%
	5	6	24%	8	32%	8	32%
	4	1	4%	3	12%	8	32%
	3			0	0%	2	8%
	2			2	8%	0	0%
	1					1	4%
	0						
	Number of pupils	25		25		25	
	Mean score	5.68		5.12		4.6	

Inference: The scale measures what the child believes others think of his class. The scores suggest the Sample Group of physically handicapped and the above average ability Control Group have a good 'other' image, whilst the below average ability Control Group scores suggest a slightly less good 'other' image, with scores of three of this group indicating a poor 'other' image.

F. Score on 'conforming versus non-conforming pupil' scale	Physically handicapped		Above average ability		Below average ability	
5	15	60%	13	52%	10	40%
4	10	40%	9	36%	9	36%
3			3	12%	3	12%
2					1	4%
1					2	8%
0						
Number of pupils	25		25		25	
Mean score	4.6		4.4		4.12	

Inference: The items forming this scale cover the range of two opposing types of behaviour. The scores of the group of physically handicapped pupils suggest almost total conforming, whilst the two Control Groups can be considered as similarly conforming. The scores suggest that three children of the below average ability group have difficulty in conforming.

G. Score on 'relationship with teacher' scale	Physically handicapped		Above average ability		Below average ability	
6	13	52%	12	48%	9	36%
5	7	28%	5	20%	6	24%
4	4	16%	7	28%	3	12%
3	1	4%	1	4%	2	8%
2					3	12%
1					2	8%
0						
Number of pupils	25		25		25	
Mean score	5.28		5.12		4.4	

Inference: This scale emphasizes the teacher's perceived degree of concern for the child. The scores suggest the physically handicapped pupils perceive their teacher relationship as the more positive, and almost all the group consider they have a good relationship with their teachers. Seven of the below average ability group consider their relationship with the teacher is much less positive.

H.	Score on 'anxiety in the classroom' scale	Physically handicapped		Above average ability		Below average ability	
Range of score	6	0	0%	0	0%	0	0%
	5	0	0%	6	24%	0	0%
	4	12	48%	12	48%	7	28%
	3	7	28%	2	8%	11	44%
	2	4	16%	5	20%	3	12%
	1	2	8%	0	0%	4	16%
	0						
	Number of pupils	25		25		25	
	Mean score	3.16		3.76		2.84	

Inference: This scale is concerned with the child's anxieties, fears and worries in the classroom. The scores of the physically handicapped pupils are nearer to the scores of the below average ability Control Group, and suggest anxiety and a lack of confidence. The scores of the above average ability group suggest concerns rather than fear or worry.

I.	Score on 'social adjustment' scale	Physically handicapped		Above average ability		Below average ability	
Range of score	5	12	48%	15	60%	8	32%
	4	11	44%	9	36%	12	48%
	3	2	8%	1	4%	1	4%
	2					3	12%
	1					1	4%
	0						
	Number of pupils	25		25		25	
	Mean score	4.4		4.56		3.92	

Inference: This scale measures the child's ability to 'get on' with other pupils in his class. The scores of the physically handicapped and above average ability pupils indicate reasonably good relationships with classmates, and just 4 below average ability pupils' scores suggest a poor relationship.

J.	Score on 'academic self image' scale	Physically handicapped		Above average ability		Below average ability	
	17–18	10	40%	16	64%	8	32%
	15–16	9	36%	7	28%	6	24%
	13–14	1	4%	2	8%	4	16%
Range of score	11–12	3	12%	0	0%	3	12%
	9–10	2	8%	0	0%	2	8%
	7–8	0	0%	0	0%	2	8%
	5–6	0	0%	0	0%	0	0%
	3–4						
	1–2						
	0						
	Number of pupils	25		25		25	
	Mean score	15.76		17.12		14.72	

Inference: This self-image scale reflects self in terms of school work. As might be expected, the group of above average ability pupils have scores which indicate a good academic self-image. The scores of the physically handicapped group indicate a favourable all-round academic self-image, as do those of the majority of the below average ability group. Four of the latter group appear to have only a fair academic self-image.

The general impression gained, therefore, from talking to individual children in the Sample Group, and observing them in the survey schools, was one of considerable self-confidence. The physically handicapped pupils were totally at ease in general discussion, and answered questions confidently and competently. Non-communicating pupils were occasional exceptions. Because of the involvement of a range of professional agencies in their lives, and those of their families, from a relatively early age, physically handicapped children are used to conversing with adults, and meeting a variety of people from different walks of life, which promotes self-confidence. This was noticeable, particularly, amongst the younger members of the sample group, and there was evidence of the 'cocktail party syndrome' amongst the five young spina bifida pupils. The scores achieved by the older physically handicapped pupils in the Sample Group, in the *Barker Lunn Children's Attitude Scales*, complement these observations, and indicate their levels of confidence and maturity are comparable with those of the above average ability Control Group. It is encouraging to note further from these scores, that in the main, the mean scores of the physically handicapped Sample Group were higher than the mean scores of the Control Groups, and no mean scores of the Sample Group were below the mean scores of the below average ability group.

8
Attainment and Achievement

The major task of this study was to ascertain whether severely physically handicapped pupils in mainstream schools might achieve a standard of academic attainment comparable with the standard achieved by the majority of their non-handicapped peers.

Some years ago, the majority of children selected for integration were considered to be more intellectually able and less physically handicapped, and attention was drawn to these two factors by Kellmer Pringle and Fiddes (1970) in relation to thalidomide children, and by Tew and Laurence (1972) in relation to children with spina bifida. Other studies by Anderson (1973), Cope and Anderson (1977) and Tew and Laurence (1978), however, examined the levels of academic attainment achieved by the severely physically handicapped and those less intellectually able, by virtue of their learning disabilities associated with handicap. Later studies by Howarth (1979), Jones (1980) and Chazan et al (1980) have sought to determine, in relation to the integration of non-selective groups of physically handicapped pupils, the respective levels of academic achievement, in response to the recommendations of the Warnock Committee. The present study gives consideration to the levels of attainment and achievement which might be reasonably expected from three distinct forms of integrated educational provision, given additional resources and support services, as described in earlier chapters.

The physically handicapped children in the Sample Group in this study are all classified as severely handicapped, and two-thirds of the children, approximately 31 in number, have associated learning difficulties. Attainment was monitored over a period of one academic year, in the skills of reading and mathematics, and the achievements of both the Sample Group of physically handicapped children, and their corresponding Control Groups, are discussed. It is reasonable to assume that the majority of handicapped children in this Sample Group are receiving through the medium of integration, a much wider educational programme at a successful level, despite individual limitations and restrictions imposed by the handicapping conditions. The previous chapter showed that socially, emotionally and behaviourally, individual progress was being achieved at a normal level.

Parental satisfaction

From the information given in the questionnaire for families and interviews, 84 per cent of the parents have indicated satisfaction with their handicapped child's progress in the mainstream primary school. In an attempt to discover how realistic the parental assessment of their children's abilities were, their ratings were compared with similar data provided by the class teachers. The results are shown in Table 8.1.

Table 8.1   Overall ability – teacher and parent assessments

| Rating | *Physically handicapped: Number of children* (N=50) | |
	Teacher assessment	Parental assessment
Above average	14	9
About average	18	18
Little below average	8	10
Making slow progress	9	7
Don't know	1	6
Totals	50	50

There was a close correspondence in the teacher and parent ratings, the same children being picked out as 'about average', although parents were slightly less likely to give their children an 'above average' rating.

Teachers were also asked how satisfied they were with the children's progress: in 32 cases they were 'satisfied', and in 12 cases, 'reasonably satisfied'. In six other cases (which have already been discussed in Chapter 4), the teachers were concerned about the slow rate of progress.

Major functional effect of handicap

In studies of this kind, it is essential to acknowledge the severity of handicap and assess, objectively, the degree of severity in relation to the major functional effect of the handicap. Is severity of handicap an important factor in determining the success or failure of a pupil in various aspects of school life and, indeed, does this determine whether that pupil is ideally placed in the mainstream school. The Sample Group of physically handicapped children were assessed in terms of the major functions which were impaired, to establish the major functional effect of their handicaps. This is a factor of considerable importance in assessing the success of the individual child's attainment and achievements in a programme of integrated education. Five distinct areas emerged from the fieldwork undertaken in the schools, and these areas are identified in Table 8.2, illustrating the area of impairment for each pupil which presents the major restriction in respect of performance in the classroom.

Table 8.2 Major functional effect of handicap

| Impairment | Sample Group | |
	Number	Percentage
Mobility	23	46%
Incontinence	11	22%
Neurological Abnormalities	10	20%
Hand Control	4	8%
Communication Skills	2	4%
Totals	50	100%

Of the 23 pupils with impaired mobility, 20 regularly used a wheelchair. Although the presence of associated learning difficulties was found in 34 pupils in the Sample Group, only in ten of the pupils was this impairment found to have a major functional effect on classroom performance, and, in every case, this was due to neurological abnormalities. The data collected suggested this as an area of related importance in this particular study, as considerable concern was expressed by class teachers, in relation to the achievement and attainment levels of pupils with special educational needs. Although only two of the pupils in the Sample Group were unable to communicate verbally, a further nine pupils had moderate speech impairments which required regular speech therapy. In all but one case, this was provided. Incontinence problems are generally felt to lead to difficulties in mainstream school placement, but the study found little evidence of this. The majority of incontinent pupils were able to deal, quite independently, with this problem, and the incontinence was generally controlled by daily routine management, or by the use of various appliances, following appropriate surgery. Where regular ancillary help was required, was amongst the very young pupils of first school age, who were still in the process of being trained, and in the survey schools where toileting facilities were not purpose built.

Influencing factors

Although severity of handicap is suggested by this study to have some effect on attainment level, it was not considered a factor of any significant importance in determining the success of the integrated provision. Social class did not influence or distract from the academic success of the Sample Group, yet family size did contradict the findings of similar studies, given that it appeared neither to influence nor limit attainment and the position of the handicapped child in the family bore no relationship to the level of attainment. The size of the class was considered to have relative importance, particularly at first school level, where an element of regular and consistent individual attention was deemed essential, especially in the task of the early assessment and identification of special educational needs.

It is pertinent to examine the classroom groupings within the survey schools, and the criteria for the admission of physically handicapped pupils to these groups. It is of interest to note that with regard to these two aspects, the nine survey schools, and the integration programmes which they offer, fall into three distinct groups. The concept of the integration programme offered by schools *C*, *E* and *F* rests on the principle of non-selective integration, embracing severely physically handicapped pupils of all levels of ability, including those with learning difficulties, in mixed ability classes within each year group. Each school has a special resource class for pupils with special needs, which serves as a base for the assessment of problems associated with learning. In addition to meeting the needs of the physically handicapped, it offers specialist teaching facilities to all pupils of the school, as and when the need for specialist attention arises. The pupils with special needs are registered with a class and an individual timetable is planned so that they remain with their group to participate in class activities, wherever possible. They may receive individual help within the class situation or may be withdrawn for specialist attention in the resource class. The number of physically handicapped pupils in the special resource classes in schools *E* and *F* is matched with an equal number of non-handicapped pupils, some of whom may require specialist teaching help. At the time of the practical investigation, although a number of pupils with special needs were placed in the special resource class in school *C*, none were physically handicapped.

Schools *B*, *H* and *I* are linked with adjoining special schools for the physically handicapped, as part of a campus situation. The schools receive handicapped pupils on a sessional basis, and ongoing assessment during such periods leads to full-time integration of physically handicapped pupils as and when appropriate. Such a system, therefore, initially embraces the concept of locational integration, which develops to afford opportunities for social and functional integration, for as many handicapped pupils as possible. The schools organize classes on the basis of vertical grouping and each school has a smaller class for pupils with special needs. It is relevant to note that no physically handicapped children in the Sample Group were placed in these classes. Selective programmes of integration were in operation in schools *A*, *D* and *G*. The three schools had all been approached by the parents of the handicapped pupils, and schools *A* and *D*, by the headteacher of the local special school for physically handicapped children. After appropriate liaison with the headteachers of the three schools, direct requests for placement were made by the parents to the LEA who discussed such placement with the headteachers of schools *A*, *D* and *G*, before final agreement was reached. In school *G*, the classes are largely based on age, but pupils with special needs are given the opportunity to work in small groups with the headteacher, or in some other organizational pattern, as staffing allows. Mixed ability grouping in respect of classroom organization is used in schools *A* and *D*.

Performance

Chapter 2 has already outlined how the criteria for the admission of pupils with physical handicaps to the survey schools, influences the type of integration programme which the schools offer. The data arising from the fieldwork of this study indicated that the performance of severely physically handicapped pupils was poorer in non-selective programmes of integration, and that this performance was related to ability level, as estimated by teachers. In relation to backwardness, Leach and Raybould (1977), Laslett (1979) and Ainscow and Tweddle(1979) associated underachievement with the presence of behaviour disorders, and this study indicated amongst 18 per cent of the Sample Group of physically handicapped pupils, a relationship between these two factors, particularly in schools *E* and *F*, situated in an industrial area with a high level of unemployment, and in schools *C* and *B*, integrating pupils from multicultural backgrounds in poor socio-economic areas associated with problems of cultural diversity. Haskell (1972) and Tobin *et al* (1981) have suggested that anxiety may impede a high level of attainment in mathematics, and this study indicated, as did that of Cope and Anderson (1977) and Carr *et al* (1983) that where a high level of mathematical ability was present, those pupils were not described as of nervous or anxious disposition. However, teachers' opinions and comments indicated that where emotional problems and signs of social immaturity were present in pupils, mathematical skills were retarded, and thus the pupils might be described as 'underachieving'.

NFER Basic Mathematics Test

It is important to consider the educational progress of physically handicapped pupils attending mainstream schools, in relation to the progress of their non-handicapped peers. The results of the NFER Basic Mathematics Tests undertaken with the Sample Group of physically handicapped pupils and the Control Groups of non-handicapped pupils are presented in graph form. The graphs show the scores of each member of the Sample and Control Groups within the age range of the test, and indicate a favourable position for the physically handicapped pupils, within the extremes of the Control Group scores.

Note: A:Pupils, non-handicapped, above average ability[*]
          B: Physically handicapped pupils
          C: Pupils, non-handicapped, below average ability[*]

[*]Teachers estimates: these should be regarded as a rough guide of children's intellectual abilities. The results shown are not to be interpreted as a precise rating scale.

In Test A, the scores show great diversity in levels of achievement and attainment amongst both the physically handicapped pupils and their non-handicapped peers, within the age range 6.9 to 8.6 years. In two cases physically handicapped pupils were unable to attempt the test due to restrictions of handicap. The scores achieved in Test B suggest a closer relationship in attainment between the Sample Group and the two Control Groups. The low scores of three spina bifida pupils within the age range of 8.4 years and 9.10 years might be assumed to relate to problems of concentration and recall, associated with the handicap, particularly in the understanding of mathematical and scientific concepts.

In the main, in Test C, for pupils within the age range of 9.7 to 10.10 years, and Test DE, for pupils between 10.00 and 11.11 years of age, the scores of the physically handicapped pupils bear a greater relationship to the scores of the Control Group of pupils estimated to be of above average ability. It might be assumed from these scores that pupils with specific physical handicaps who experience difficulties in mathematical processes and relationships at an early age, are able, as a result of specialist and remedial support, to reach an average level of achievement and so maintain consistent progress. The scores suggest that learning patterns have perhaps become more established in pupils within these age ranges. Table 8.3 gives further support to these findings.

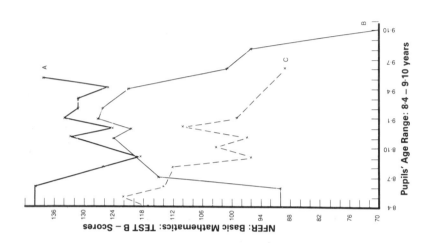

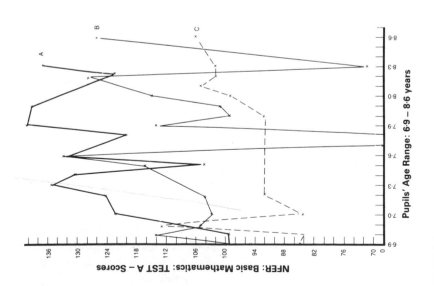

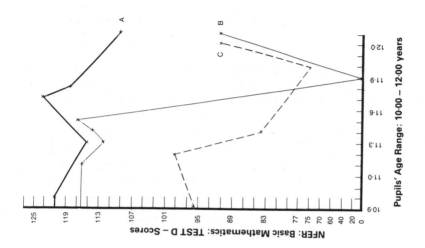

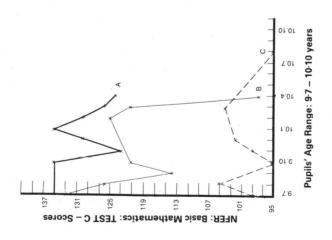

Table 8.3   NFER Basic Mathematics Tests: mean standardized scores of Sample and Control Groups

Test A:	Above Average Ability Control Group:	125.4	Mean Age:	7.14 years
N=15	Physically Handicapped Sample Group:	108.8	Mean Age:	7.12 years
	Below Average Ability Control Group:	96.7	Mean Age:	7.23 years
Test B:	Above Average Ability Control Group:	130.2	Mean Age:	8.65 years
N=11	Physically Handicapped Sample Group:	109	Mean Age:	8.76 years
	Below Average Ability Control Group:	105.9	Mean Age:	8.36 years
Test C:	Above Average Ability Control Group:	129	Mean Age:	9.76 years
N=6	Physically Handicapped Sample Group:	119.7	Mean Age:	9.49 years
	Below Average Ability Control Group:	99.8	Mean Age:	9.50 years
Test DE:	Above Average Ability Control Group:	116	Mean Age:	11.06 years
N=5	Physically Handicapped Sample Group:	109.8	Mean Age:	11.20 years
	Below Average Ability Control Group:	89.8	Mean Age:	11.05 years

Maximum standardized score for any test: 140 (as set out in the test manual)
Minimum standardized score for any test: 70 (as set out in the test manual)

It is encouraging to record that of the group of physically handicapped pupils below the age of 6.9 years, four pupils were able to attempt Test A, and achieve raw scores between 7 and 19 out of a maximum of 40.

Neale Analysis of Reading Ability

The *Neale Analysis of Reading Ability* scores, which provided a measurement of the skills in reading rate, accuracy and comprehension, of both the Sample Group of handicapped pupils and the Control Groups of non-handicapped pupils, are shown, in respect of each survey school, in the following graphs.

School C

The lowest scores amongst the physically handicapped pupils of school *C*, which has a non-selective programme of integration, in reading rate skills are indicative of severe restrictions normally associated with physical handicaps. The interesting patterns of scores indicate inconsistency in achievements in reading accuracy and comprehension skills amongst physically handicapped pupils who have not been 'selected' for integration. The pupil scoring below the 'below average ability' curve has English as a second

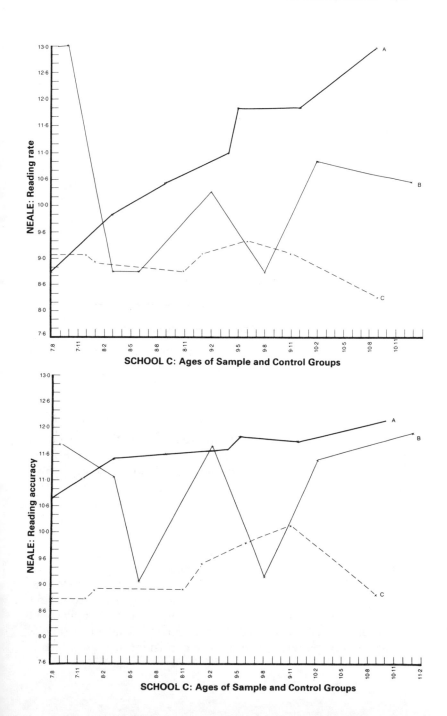

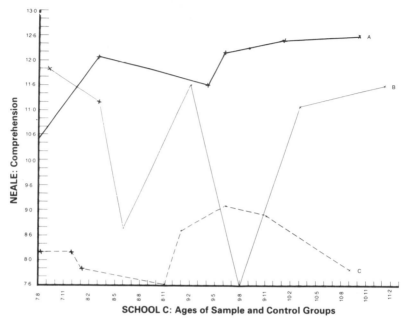

SCHOOL C: Ages of Sample and Control Groups

language. These patterns give clear indication of the wide range of ability amongst pupils with physical handicaps.

School E

A true picture of the apparent success of the integration of physically handicapped pupils is presented by school *E*. The programme of integration is non-selective, and the scores represent a wide variety of handicap and the full range of ability. The results are most encouraging, given that they show an achievement and attainment pattern for physically handicapped pupils in the skills of reading, remaining within the limits of the two extremes, maximum and minimum attainment.

In reading rate skills, an equal number of physically handicapped pupils score above the average[+] level, and below the average[-] level. The physically handicapped pupils' scores are nearer the ability level of the 'below average' pupils, but marginally better, with regard to accuracy skills. The 'above average ability' pattern shows a more consistent increase which is

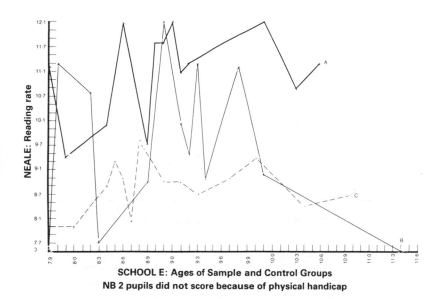

SCHOOL E: Ages of Sample and Control Groups
NB 2 pupils did not score because of physical handicap

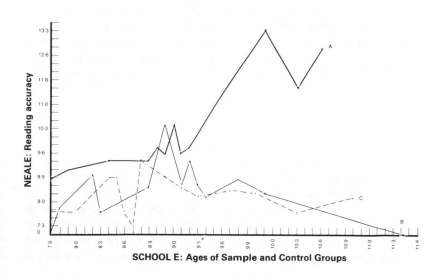

SCHOOL E: Ages of Sample and Control Groups

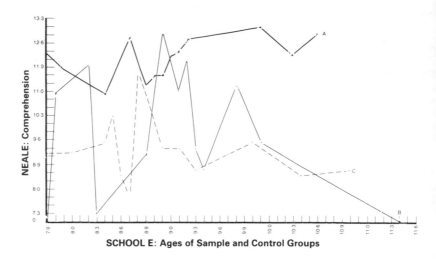

SCHOOL E: Ages of Sample and Control Groups

not obvious amongst the physically handicapped pupils' scores. It is of interest to note that the peak of the scores is reached around the middle of the age range of the handicapped pupils, and then descends in the opposite direction to the 'above average ability' pupils' scores. Such a pattern suggests the rate of achievement amongst some physically handicapped pupils reaches a ceiling earlier than amongst the non-handicapped. Can this be linked, perhaps, with the increasing severity of handicap which imposes greater restrictions on the acquiring of knowledge? In comprehension skills, the scores are low on average amongst physically handicapped pupils, and this signifies, in some cases, the lack of concentration directly associated with the handicapping condition.

School F

School *F* has a non-selective programme of integration, and its physically handicapped pupils represent a very wide range of ability, and variety of handicap. Generally, low scores or no scores attained by the handicapped pupils are possibly due to the very severe limitations of handicap. In addition, several pupils have been placed in the special resource class for assessment purposes, and therefore it can be reasonably assumed that they may not be appropriately placed in the long term. Three physically

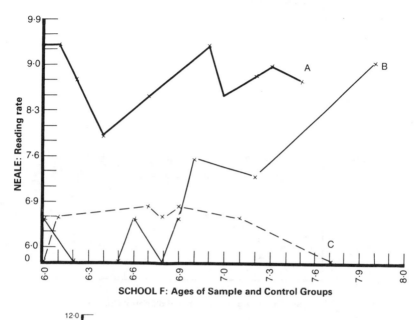

SCHOOL F: Ages of Sample and Control Groups

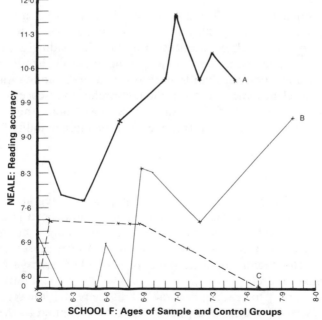

SCHOOL F: Ages of Sample and Control Groups

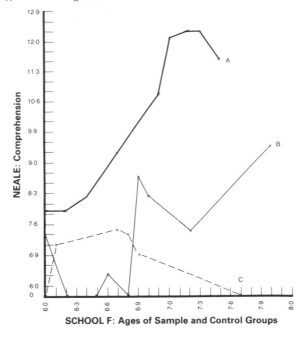

SCHOOL F: Ages of Sample and Control Groups

handicapped pupils above the age of six years were unable to achieve any scores, possibly due to the limitations of handicap and/or apparent lack of intellectual ability. In reading accuracy, there was an increase in scores amongst the physically handicapped pupils to a level higher than that of 'below average ability' pupils. There was clear indication from the comprehension scores that in the cases of seven of the physically handicapped pupils, the level of understanding is greater, at this age, than functional ability level.

School B

School *B* is selective of handicapped pupils for integration, and the two low scores achieved by physically handicapped pupils in reading rate skills are indicative of the handicapping conditions – spasticity in the throat and speech muscles, which causes speech defects. This factor might account for the below average ability performance levels.

With respect to reading accuracy skills, here the low scores of the physically handicapped pupils might be attributed to the fact

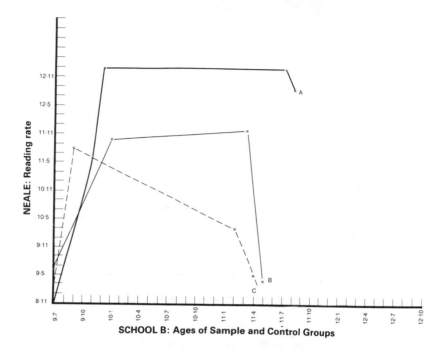

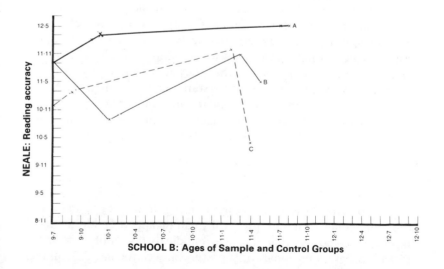

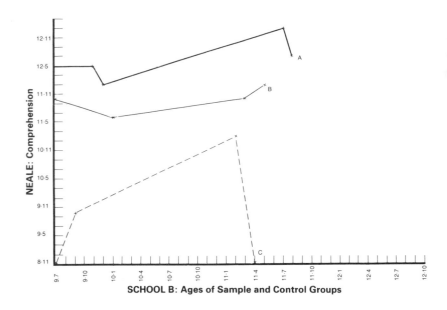

SCHOOL B: Ages of Sample and Control Groups

that for three pupils in the Sample Group, English is a second language, hence, a reduced accuracy skill, representative of pupils' below average ability level. It is relevant to note the absence of immigrant pupils in the Control Groups. The comprehension scores show a greater understanding by the three handicapped pupils in question of what they are reading, than how they are reading. These scores suggest that they have the ability to grasp the gist of the content and an understanding of meaning. Here, the physical handicap does not seem to present restrictions, and it would appear that the scores in respect of comprehension skills are a more accurate indication of ability level.

School H

School *H* participated in a campus integration programme, and the consistent scores for physically handicapped children, in all three tests, showed that physical handicap does not necessarily restrict progress or apparently present any particular difficulties, in this situation.

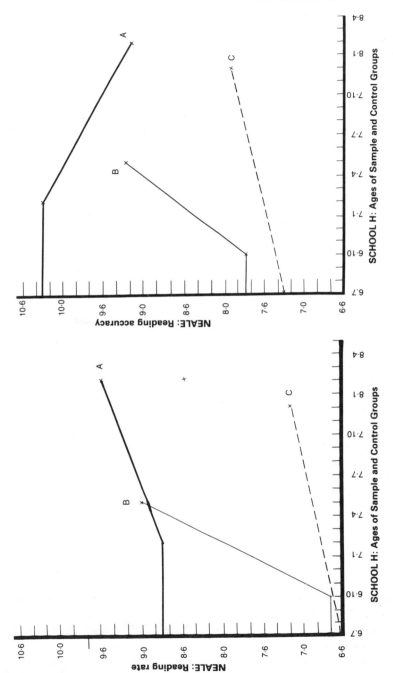

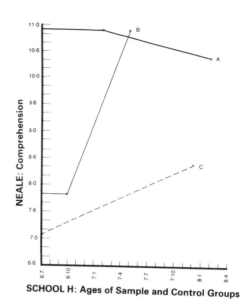

SCHOOL H: Ages of Sample and Control Groups

School I

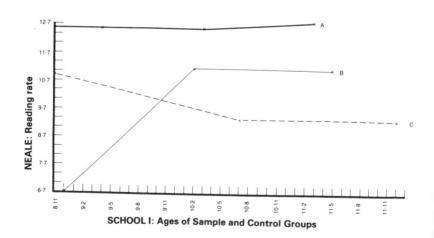

SCHOOL I: Ages of Sample and Control Groups

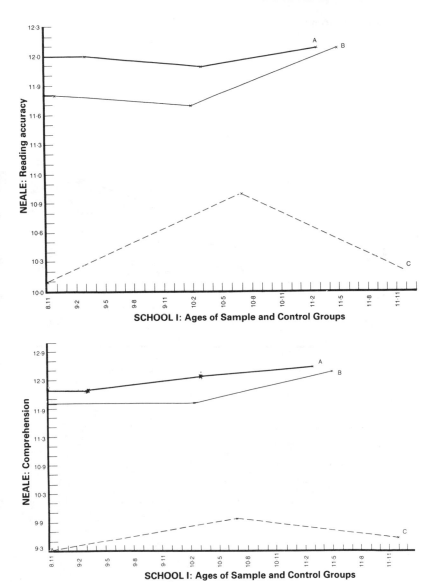

The integration programme at school *I* similarly operates, and there is some selection of physically handicapped pupils for integration. In reading rate, the low score of one handicapped pupil is possibly due to handicap – blindness in one eye and very restricted sight in the other. However, in reading accuracy and comprehension skills, the physically handicapped pupils achieved a consistent score pattern, closely related to the 'above average ability' pupils' scores.

School A

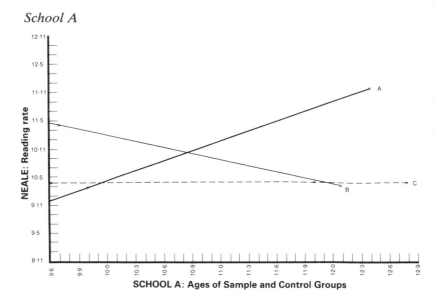

SCHOOL A: Ages of Sample and Control Groups

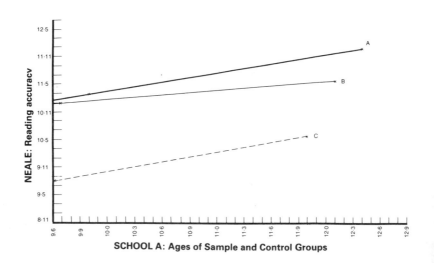

SCHOOL A: Ages of Sample and Control Groups

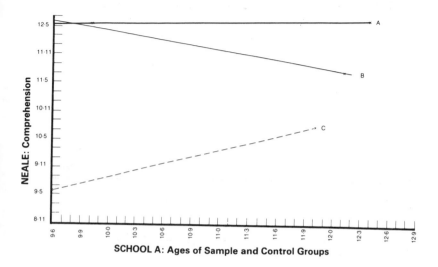

SCHOOL A: Ages of Sample and Control Groups

School *A*, which is selected by parents for their physically handicapped children, is non-selective of its special needs pupils at the present time, but would be selective if a greater number of such pupils were involved. These factors might well bear relevance to the scores.

School D

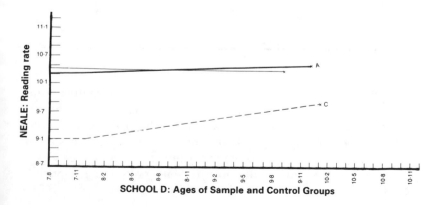

SCHOOL D: Ages of Sample and Control Groups

SCHOOL D: Ages of Sample and Control Groups

SCHOOL D: Ages of Sample and Control Groups

School *D* accommodates, in the main, pupils from multicultural backgrounds, and English as a second language is therefore a common factor. The school was selected by parents, and both physically handicapped pupils had previously attended a special school, where they were prepared for integration at a later stage. The scores achieved in all three reading skills are reasonably consistent.

School G

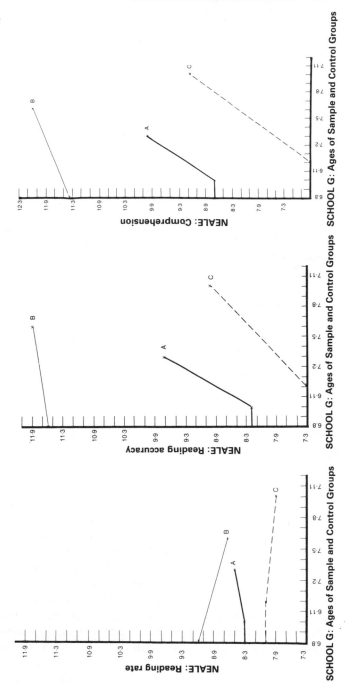

The physically handicapped pupils integrated into school *G* scored well above the average ability level of non-handicapped pupils. Integration had been achieved as a result of a private arrangement between the school, situated in a middle class area, and the parents of the handicapped pupils.

Overall, the mean standardized scores of the Sample Group and Control Groups show the scores for physically handicapped pupils falling between the scores for the Control Groups, as Table 8.4 illustrates.

Table 8.4 Neale Analysis of Reading Ability: mean standardized scores of Sample and Control Groups

Reading rate		*Mean age*
Above Average Ability Control Group:	10.4 years	8.37 years
Physically Handicapped Sample Group:	8.95 years	8.30 years
Below Average Ability Control Group:	8.55 years	8.45 years
Reading accuracy		
Above Average Ability Control Group:	10.22 years	8.37 years
Physically Handicapped Sample Group:	9.01 years	8.30 years
Below Average Ability Control Group:	8.13 years	8.45 years
Comprehension		
Above Average Ability Control Group:	11.48 years	8.37 years
Physically Handicapped Sample Group:	9.49 years	8.30 years
Below Average Ability Control Group:	8.40 years	8.45 years

Evaluation of resources

From data obtained, and subsequent standardized test results, from discussion with staff and parents, and the pupils themselves, significant evidence emerges to support the view that severely physically handicapped pupils placed in mainstream schools can and do reach levels of achievement and attainment despite the restrictions imposed by handicap, which are favourably comparable with those reached by non-handicapped pupils. Generally it was felt by teachers and parents alike that progress was better than might have been achieved in a special school, that the avenues of opportunities available to the handicapped pupils, both academically and socially, were measurably wider, and the pupils' individual levels of potential were positively extended. The pupils' special educational needs were adequately met and well provided for, and associated learning difficulties were catered for through the medium of additional specialist resources. However, two factors of some influence which contributed to successful integration were identified. Extra teaching resources and favourable staff – pupil ratios are essential, and the percentage of pupils with special needs in relation to the general population of the host school must be carefully balanced to ensure that the school reflects a true image of the society in which the handicapped will eventually take their place.

There is a basic requirement for a considerable input of resources into mainstream schools, to enable them to meet a wide range of special needs. Specialist teachers and ancillary staff are the major resources for an integration programme. Hegarty and Pocklington (1982) suggest that 'one way of providing the necessary specialist expertise in the ordinary classroom is to appoint teachers in a support role' to provide back-up for the work of the class teacher, by helping the pupil with special needs to understand lesson content, and carrying out appropriate preparatory and follow-up work. The headteachers of the nine survey schools held broadly similar opinions about the desirability of specialist teaching help, but practice in the survey schools varied greatly. Schools *C, D, E, F, G* and *H* felt that specialist help, particularly in reading skills, was beneficial to pupils with special needs, but only two schools, *E* and *F*, felt the most practical way was in the form of special resource classes. The headteachers of schools *A, B* and *I* were strongly opposed to withdrawal. They felt this defeated the entire principle of integration, and intimated they would arrange for specialist help to be given in the classroom. Schools *C, E* and *F* had a specialist teaching room and equipment which included language masters, word processors, and electric possum typewriters, with spelling and sentence making boards, and school *D* had a language laboratory. Schools *B, D* and *I* felt that extra teaching assistance was not required, but the headteachers of schools *G* and *H* said they gave remedial help to slow learning pupils, but not to the physically handicapped pupils as this was not necessary at the present time.

The headteacher of school *C* described how she employed a specialist teacher of English as a second language, to give specialist language work to those pupils for whom English was a second language, including physically handicapped pupils. This specialist work was reinforced by ancillary staff who spent time in conversation with the pupils and helped them with their reading. The specialist support teacher with responsibility for the resource class in school *F* suggested that her primary role was to facilitate and promote the handicapped pupils' assimilation into the specialist resource class, and to introduce him or her into school life generally, by encouraging non-handicapped pupils to include their handicapped peers in classroom activities, explaining some of the child's difficulties associated with the handicap, and intervening over initial misunderstandings and embarrassing situations. The specialist and support teacher working within school *C* pointed out that she sought to provide the requisite support, within the classroom situation, wherever feasible, and this required an assessment of learning situations, in order to decide when to intervene with explanation or reinforcement, and when to remain in the background. Over-supporting can lead to a situation of over-dependence on the support teacher, by the pupil with special needs, running the risk of isolation rather than integration. A further role for the experienced support teacher, highly relevant to integration, is in assisting class teachers to develop skills appropriate to meeting pupils' special needs. This requires an ability to diagnose a particular learning difficulty or area of learning difficulty, and the expertise to determine how to provide the necessary remediation. Hegarty and Pocklington (1981) stress the critical importance of encouraging the class teacher:

> to feel that he or she has an active role to play. This may entail a didactic or at least persuading role: getting the teacher to see the need to modify teaching content or approach, helping him to simplify learning tasks and implement a suitable programme of work geared to the individual pupil's needs.

The general feeling conveyed by the headteachers of the nine survey schools was that all children with special needs should be taught in mainstream classrooms wherever possible. The headteacher of school *I* suggested that withdrawal or special resource classes separate children and come to be regarded as undesirable by those who believe in educating all children together, which, he further suggested, was the purpose of integration. One head-teacher, of school *B*, expressed the view that she would like to make extra specialist provision, in addition to what the school provided at present for the physically handicapped pupils, for the 15–20 per cent of other pupils with special educational needs. This view was unanimously supported by the headteachers of the other eight survey schools, who all agreed they would need extra resources in terms of staffing, equipment and materials, to make this provision. The headteachers of schools *A*, *E* and *H* suggested that suitably qualified and experienced teachers might prove of more intrinsic value in the provision of extra specialist help, than either specialist advice or ancillary help.

The findings presented in this chapter, and in the preceding chapter, suggest that the majority of the Sample Group of physically handicapped children in this study are receiving through the special educational provision examined, an education which it would seem meets their special needs, both academically and socially. Special provision in the form of adequate resources and appropriate support services are essential contributions towards the levels of achievement and attainment reached, in the various integration programmes, organized by the nine survey schools.

Part IV

Policy Implications

9
A Consideration of Integrated Education

Anderson (1973) suggested that the most rewarding aspect of the many visits which she had made to schools integrating physically handicapped children was a new and first-hand appreciation of what was possible. By 1983, much of what was possible in 1973 had begun, and the Education Act 1981, which became law on 1st April 1983, gave official approval to the integration of the maximum number of pupils with special educational needs, in mainstream schools. Given the special resources and support services which this study has described, it is possible to offer severely physically handicapped children, including those with associated learning difficulties, an education in a mainstream school, which is both academically and socially viable. Now that a national commitment to the concept of integration is accepted there has been a substantial increase in the number of children with special needs being educated in mainstream schools. Facilities comparable with those at present provided in special schools must be made available to meet those pupils' special educational needs. The study has discussed a number of arrangements whereby professional interaction between the different specialist agencies has opened up new possibilities to the parents, teachers, psychologists and others involved in meeting special needs. Greater exploitation of the different perspectives which the professions bring to integration, is vital in order to further the integration of physically handicapped children within the community, by making mainstream schools special.

This conclusion emerges from looking at actual programmes of integration, and what was achieved within them. The starting point was the presence of pupils with special needs in mainstream schools, and the determination of, and subsequent examination of, a number of factors that might be considered to contribute to the successful operation of programmes of integration.

This section discusses the policy implications which have been highlighted by the practical investigation, and the impact of recent legislation.

Establishing the provision

If provision is flexibly geared to meeting the differing needs of each individual child, then placement must be influenced through consideration given to the general well-being of the child. However it may not be feasible to provide more than one viable option. The need for such provision strengthens the case for integration and indicates the essentiality of further development of more integrated forms of provision, to enable more handicapped children to be educated within the mainstream school system. The maximum possible participation in all aspects of school life, both educational and social, is the ultimate aim of integration. However, emphasis must be given to the benefits of social interaction, where the success of the relationships which are fostered can promote a caring attitude and acceptance of handicap. Placing a physically handicapped child in a mainstream school is an idea particularly acceptable to parents of handicapped children, and regardless of the degree of integration, this presence greatly facilitates the possibility of transferring individual children into more integrated programmes. Hence, the opportunities for daily interaction with non-handicapped children are greatly in advance of those provided, if any, by isolated special schools, and integration into local mainstream schools can promote integration within the community.

When the handicapped child is a member of a mainstream school, non-handicapped children act as a constant challenge and stimulus. Such stimulus provides greater achievement in all aspects of school life. The wider range of specialized resources, better staffing ratios, more specialized care and attention accepted as essential special school resources, must be made available to the mainstream school.

The study has identified staff of schools as the central resource in an integration programme, and shown that integration is not simply a question of educating those pupils formally assigned to the integration programme. The new roles required of staff involved in integration need to be clearly defined and an increase in staffing provision necessary to accommodate the extension of these roles is essential.

Teacher attitudes are affected in significant ways by how the integrated provision is established and by the level of teacher involvement in the initial establishment. Where staff are involved in early discussions and consultations, it is obvious that the integration programme is clearly acknowledged as a matter for the whole school, and one which effects major changes there. Furthermore, although the majority of staff working in the survey schools are supportive of, and committed to, the principle of integration, it is a matter for concern to find evidence of staff not being consulted in some measure on a major development in the life of the school.

An important factor in the success of integrated education is the amount and quality of guidance available from external agencies. In order that all children's special educational needs might be recognized, and realistically catered for in the appropriate educational setting, extensive resources and a firm commitment on the part of the LEA and the community health service are essential prerequisites. Attitudes of both staff and pupils towards the integration of pupils with special needs, and the assimilation of a special provision into the school, can be substantially influenced when the adequate provision of adequate resources provides a stimulating learning environment. The extent of such an influence is reflected in the educational environments within the nine survey schools, and resources are an obvious contributory factor to success. By examining the different forms of provision in terms of staffing and supportive services, premises, resources and transportation, the influence of provision is determined. One conclusion which emerges from such an exercise is that comparisons between integrated and segregated provision in terms of cost, suggest that the popularly held belief about the relative cheapness of integration does not have a sound basis. A number of factors must be considered when establishing the provision:

(a) Integration should mean a process whereby a mainstream school and a group of pupils with special needs, interact to make a new educational whole;

(b) Integration must not be seen to concern only the handicapped, whose success is assured when they are assimilated into a mainstream school; this implies it is something which is *done* by the handicapped;

(c) An existing concept of integration is associated with a number of misconceptions about special educational provision. The two per cent of the total school population, who formally receive special education either in special schools or in special classes, is the group usually in mind when integration is at issue;

(d) A high percentage of pupils with less serious needs, who are already in mainstream schools, are considered not eligible for integration! Pupils need to be ascertained for special education in a uniform way and schools must first make adequate provision for these existing members of the school population. Such a distinction makes an element of sense, when integration extends what the mainstream school is already providing, to enable the more severely handicapped pupil to be provided for as well.

At the present time, the extent to which pupils are deemed in need of special education varies widely from authority to authority, and what is recognized as a special educational need depends in part on local provision.

Variety and range of special educational provisions recommended

Whilst it is impossible to cater for every combination of individual needs it is recognized that as great a variety of organizational arrangements as practicable should be available. The Warnock Report listed the range of provision which the Committee believed would be needed in future for pupils with special educational needs:

(i) full-time education in an ordinary class with any necessary help and support;

(ii)   education in an ordinary class with periods of withdrawal to a special class or unit or other supporting base;

(iii)   education in a special class or unit with periods of attendance at an ordinary class and full involvement in the general community life and extra-curricular activities of the ordinary school;

(iv)   full-time education in the special class or unit with social contact with the main school;

(v)   education in a special school, day or residential, with some shared lessons with a neighbouring ordinary school;

(vi)   full-time education in a day special school with social contact with an ordinary school;

(vii)   full-time education in a residential school with social contact with an ordinary school;

(viii)   short-term education in hospitals and other establishments;

(ix)   long-term education in hospitals and other establishments; and

(x)   home tuition.

Some children may need to attend a special school for some period in their early school life, and specialist help at this stage may well enable them to complete their education, at a later stage, in a mainstream school. However the majority of children with special needs are on the rolls of mainstream schools and have their special educational needs identified and met through the school's own endeavours and resources.

The schools within which physically handicapped children are placed must be selected with care. The extent to which the school is able to meet the special needs of pupils, will be influenced by its organization and by its ability to adapt to new demands. The school community as a whole, will have its own approach to the integration of children with special needs, and this must be established before integration begins. Of essential importance is an awareness by the whole school, of special educational needs, and the development of constructive and positive attitudes, towards the achievement of progress and independence for the handicapped pupil.

The school will need to consider a number of factors when planning integrated provision. Teachers' attitudes, organizational skills and the general deployment of staff are key issues and the role of the mainstream school in integration is greatly influenced by the importance of a favourable staff – pupil ratio. The use of non-teaching staff support is important as a means of achieving staffing ratios which facilitate smaller classes in general and small teaching groups in particular, and give greater access to the whole curriculum.

The more marked an individual child's special educational needs in terms of intellectual disability, the progressively more difficult it is for the child to learn in association with his non-handicapped peers. Thus, some pupils' needs call for placement in a special school or in a special unit associated with a mainstream school, where the appropriate curriculum can be provided. However, every care must be taken to promote some social integration with children in the mainstream school. The potential for conflict exists when parents want for their child a level of integration which is not easy to effect or when the range of provision within the LEA does not include the type of provision which would be the most appropriate for a particular child.

The problems in practice

There are serious difficulties with the concept of integration that call its usefulness into question. Integration may be used to mean different things, yet it is a means, not an end in itself, and pupils with special needs require education not integration. The primary concern is development in all its aspects, and other considerations, such as where the education takes place, have relevance only in relation to it. If integration is seen as a good idea in its own right, unfortunate consequences may result. Pupils with special educational needs are not necessarily at an advantage when placed in mainstream schools, and the unsuitability and inappropriateness of integration arrangements can result in failed educational provision. This restricts the opinions of those who seek to advocate integration, and as a consequence causes others to refuse to consider any form of integration. If pupils were ascertained for special education in a uniform way and schools made adequate provision for the 18 per cent of pupils with special educational needs already in the school, then integration would extend what the mainstream school was already providing, to allow the more severely handicapped to be provided for as well.

The difference in the learning environment leads to different constraints and opportunities for pupils with special needs. Some innovative practices for supporting such pupils within the mainstream classroom situation emerge from the practical investigation. Teachers require the incentive to provide the necessary support in an unobtrusive and cost-effective way, enabling the pupil to have access to the lesson without being isolated from peers. Integration programmes entail the modification of teaching practice, and the difficulties which emerge in this area stem in part from lack of training and lack of information from, and in consultation with, specialist agencies, hence a lack of appropriate strategies for managing the learning processes of pupils with special needs in mainstream classes.

Importantly, the findings of the study suggest that the major functional effect of the physical handicap is a vital factor in the levels of attainment and achievement, which might be expected from integration. The majority of pupils in the sample group were dually or multipli-handicapped, and many experienced areas of difficulty directly associated with the handicapping condition, which affected management and performance within the classroom environment. This, in turn, imposed curriculum restrictions. Such factors no doubt influenced the decision to delineate categories of handicap, and the rethinking of the nature of special educational needs. The study examined special provision for handicapped pupils with intellectual as well as physical impairments in mainstream schools; in mainstream classes; in mainstream classes with the necessary extra help; through a special resouce withdrawal system, and the basing of children in a special resource class within the school. The choice seems to depend considerably on the proportion of severely physically handicapped pupils within the total physically handicapped pupil group. The study shows, however, that physically handicapped pupils of relatively low ability achieve better and their academic performance is best, when the teacher does not regard them as slow learners, and so treats them as ordinary members of the class.

Programmes of integration involve a wide range of professionals from outside the school. The investigation focused particularly on LEA support, the school psychological service and community health service personnel, and related aspects of professional interaction. With the exception of just a few cases their involvement with the integration programmes examined appeared to be far from satisfactory. A recurrent theme offered to explain this situation was pressures caused by understaffing and overwork. Yet, the results of the practical investigation revealed that schools were often in particular need of the specialist advice and support which might be offered in terms of a multidisciplinary approach.

Teachers involved with a programme of integration depend on external agencies for specialist advice and support, and are vulnerable in the absence of the opportunity to share their professional concerns. Generally, a move towards greater interdisciplinary co-operation is vital. The study highlighted the need for professional collaboration with colleagues of different disciplines, in order to share and collate information, disseminate skills and acquire the ability to view pupils' special educational needs in a comprehensive light. Already existing staff shortages, however, are further exacerbated by the demands of integration programmes, so although the importance of interdisciplinary interaction is acknowledged, it must be stressed that it may be an ideal difficult to achieve.

Similarly, Hegarty and Pocklington's (1981) research found that 'locating contributions from different disciplinary backgrounds within a common conceptual framework can be a challenging intellectual task' which, unless agreed and identified, can defeat efforts at interdisciplinary interaction. In the present study, only a few examples of positively developing interdisciplinary collaborations were identified, and in the main these were somewhat limited in scope, and merely emphasized assessment of special educational needs. Much greater support is required from medical, nursing and therapy services, the special education advisory service, the school psychological and child guidance services, and from social services.

Interpreting the results

Many parents regularly saw their children working in the school environment and this promoted motivation and greater interaction between home and school. Others benefited from seeing the management of their children by teachers and therapists, and were encouraged to continue treatments and extra tuition in the home environment. Home visits are positive ways of forming working relationships between home, school and specialist agencies. A variety of social and educational opportunities allowed purposeful contacts which led to a general level of befriending, and fostered amiable relationships. Formal involvement of parents in their children's education was evident in three of the nine survey schools, and foundations were being laid for a greater involvement of parents in four of the other survey schools. The parents of a handicapped child have many painful adjustments to make during the child's early years, but the findings of this study suggested that the majority of parents had made these adjustments successfully.

The extent to which mainstream class teachers endorse the presence of pupils with special needs in their schools is a crucial factor. The study highlighted this, and 90 per cent of the teachers who completed a questionnaire were in favour of physically handicapped pupils being placed at their school. It is of interest to note that 12 teachers had expressed some reluctance to the idea of an integration programme when it was first suggested, but had quite voluntarily changed their minds after experience of the programme. Most teachers willingly accepted pupils with special needs into their classes and planned appropriate programmes to aid social as well as academic achievement and attainment. Although more than half of the mainstream class teachers described their knowledge of handicap, at the outset of the integration programme, as non-existent or poor, the majority claimed a considerable increase in their knowledge following direct experience of, and contact with, pupils with special needs. The impression gained was that the majority of teachers felt their knowledge of handicap was sufficient to teach pupils with special needs because of the support available within the school, but insufficient to meet the special educational needs which presented implications for teaching in terms of classroom performance.

Teachers can contribute measurably more to the education of handicapped pupils if they are better informed and possess the requisite skills. In the three schools where specialist/advisory teachers were employed, liaison between the specialist and mainstream class teacher was generally considered to be both purposeful and constructive, and positive support and advice was evident in terms of educational achievement and social adjustment amongst pupils with special needs.

One of the wider administrative problems is the provision of better training, and retraining through in-service, for teachers, all of whom may at some time in their careers be required to teach handicapped children. Teacher training must be given priority and a special education component must be included in all initial training courses and offered also to serving teachers. Full-time or in-service courses leading to a recognized qualification are recommended, and other specific additional courses, as well as the promotion of research and development in special education. Yet there is no mention of training in the Education Act 1981, and research has shown consistently that extensive in-service training, coupled with ongoing support from other professional and advisory services, is not available.

Class teachers have to make integration work, however poorly organized the project, however ill-advised the selection of handicapped pupils, and however lacking the provision of special equipment or ancillary staff. Yet, teachers in mainstream schools are subjected to continuous pressures and criticisms and might not welcome additional tasks which may increase both. It is difficult to feel enthusiasm for changes which may put one's professional abilities to the test in unforeseen, and perhaps unchosen ways and this critical factor must be seriously considered by their administrators. Therefore, as more extensive systems of integrated education develop, a closer and more realistic liaison between specialists of all disciplines needs careful consideration and priority must be given to appropriate improvements in teacher training, and a substantially more efficient support service. The employment of an adequate number of suitably trained and experienced teachers within a programme of integration is strongly recommended, as the lack of appropriate liaison and support is apparent in schools where specialist teachers are not employed, and hence adequate systems of liaison are the exception rather than the rule.

There must be early involvement of the officer of the LEA who has been designated specific responsibility for handicapped children in the mainstream school system. His role must include the co-ordination of help for the family, by promoting contact between the parents, the school and all concerned with the placement. However, in many areas this 'named person', originally recommended by the Warnock Committee, has not yet been appointed.

Early assessment of the child's handicap, as outlined in the 1981 Act, is essential, and careful consideration requires to be given to the projected level of ability and attainment. Any specific difficulties which may arise at a later date should be advised upon and noted. Pre-school experience can aid the handicapped child's ability to integrate socially and provide an opportunity for familiarization with the host school before he begins his full-time education. Such experience will greatly enhance the handicapped child's chances of success.

The attitude of the head and staff of the host school are of essential importance. They must be fully informed about the children's handicaps and consulted at every stage. The entire staff should ideally be committed to the concept of integration, because, however good the facilities, handicapped children may well remain in isolation if the staff are not positively aiming towards a maximum degree of integration for them into the general life of the school.

The fostering of close relations between the teachers working with and the ancillary staff responsible for, children with special needs, is of critical importance. The level of staff skills, their knowledge of handicapping conditions and their ability to appraise specific learning difficulties associated with the various disabilities, will enhance the success of the integrated provision. The assistance of the whole staff is essential to gain confidence in assessing the level of expectation amongst handicapped children. They must endeavour to recognize the need for encouragement and support, without destroying effort towards independence and be able to provide skilled help to assist pupils to overcome learning difficulties, and feelings of inadequacy and frustration, caused by the limitations of physical disabilities.

Results from the analysis of the data revealed that the shortage of resources, supporting services and ancillary staff, the inaccessibility of mainstream school buildings, and the attitudes of the various agencies concerned, are chiefly the reasons for the absence of active integration. The fact that there is still a dearth of these essential facilities strengthens the case for integration. It recommends the need for a marked expansion in the resources devoted to the provision of educational help in order to enable the integration of a greater number of severely physically handicapped children in mainstream schools to become a reality. Ideally, accommodation for physically handicapped pupils within the main-stream school should be purpose-built, and facilities in addition to classrooms should include a medical room, special toileting facilities, a room for therapy, and a small quiet room/rooms which can be made available to visiting specialist personnel, and for specialist help for pupils. It is suggested that some mileage may be achieved through opportunities for full discussions with other LEAs who have had experience in making provision of a similar kind, and also with special schools.

The extent to which the school is able to meet the special needs of pupils is influenced by its organization and by its ability to adapt to new demands. The major function of the curriculum in integration is to provide for the educational needs of the handicap-ped pupil, and it is important to distinguish between the entire curriculum of a school, and the effective curriculum for the pupils with special needs from which their programmes of work are selected. The two opposing principles on which the curriculum in integration rests are the opportunity to give handicapped pupils the same or similar access to the curriculum as their non-handicapped peers, and the provision of appropriate help to meet their special needs to enable them to take full advantage of the curriculum on offer. It is essential to apply these principles and find a balance between them.

The findings of this study show how the correct balance has been achieved by some schools by capitalizing on the curricular opportunities presented by school organization, and providing individual programmes of work for pupils with special needs, within that framework. Integration is a matter for the whole school, and the expertise of specialist/support staff is relevant only in the curriculum development necessary to meet the special needs. Class teachers need to work in conjunction with specialist teachers to ensure the full range of the curriculum is available for pupils with special needs, and to devise new curricular components different from those already in the school, appropriate for the meeting of such needs.

The monitoring of pupils' progress assumes particular importance in integration, especially when pupils are receiving inputs from different sources, and a co-ordination of achievements and attainments is essential. The practical investigation produced some worthwhile examples of assessment and record-keeping, used effectively and purposefully in the schools. Attention is drawn to the fact that teachers must essentially have the ability to collate their acquired knowledge through direct experience, for curricular purposes, and as a source of information for colleagues and other professionals concerned with the child with special needs. As was clearly illustrated in the findings from two survey schools (schools *F* and *H*), records that were devised and maintained with pupils' educational programmes in mind were a means of monitoring their educational progress which, in turn, ensured that inputs in the form of additional resources and support services combined to form coherent educational programmes.

Social and emotional dimensions

The maximum possible participation in all aspects of social life is the ultimate aim of integration, but emphasis must be given to the benefit of social interaction where the relationships fostered can promote a caring attitude towards the handicap and ultimately an acceptance of it. From the practical investigation emerged examples such as changing the time of morning assembly, ensuring all pupils had a common break-time, and arranging school transport to enable pupils with special needs to begin and end the school day with their non-handicapped peers. There was some evidence of the successful use of peer-tutoring, which is widespread in the USA, but generally used with more caution here. When the handicapped child first arrived at school, he was matched with a non-handicapped child during the first term, an arrangement which gradually subsided as the child made friends and became accustomed to, and more confident in, the classroom way of life.

The overall impression gained was, that at primary school level the amount and quality of social integration between handicapped and non-handicapped children is very encouraging. In terms of social and emotional development, there was a broad consensus of opinion amongst teachers, parents and pupils themselves that pupils with special needs had benefited from integrated provision. Ninety per cent of the parents of the 50 handicapped children considered that their children were very happy at school, and this view was largely confirmed by parents of the Control Groups, teachers, and by my own personal observations. There were measurable gains in self-confidence and independence amongst pupils with special needs, and their presence had achieved, amongst their non-handicapped peers, a realistic acceptance of the individual handicapping conditions. Friendly and positive relationships occurred quite naturally, and only occasionally involved outgroups within the school. This involvement, however, was considered advantageous to both groups, in that it met, equally, a variety of special needs to be found amongst the pupil population of a mainstream school.

Negative relationships, such as teasing, were comparatively rare, and there was little or no evidence of untoward behaviour and bizarre mannerisms. This is not to deny the existence of problems in social relationships, however, and some differences were noted in friendship patterns, according to the nature of the handicap. However, friendship choices did not appear to be affected by the severity of handicap, or by the actual functions which were impaired, and no physically handicapped pupils were social isolates. Such findings are encouraging, and bear relative value to pupils' social and emotional development in integration programmes. A number of factors – age, nature of special needs, kind of interaction taking place, level of supervision and staff support, and opportunities for independent action – interact in a complex way with each other, and are influenced by the characteristics of the individual locations, and the pupils within them. The study identified the importance of such factors, and focused attention on the determinants of social and emotional development, so analysing the social milieu of integration programmes.

Attainment and achievement

The attainment and achievement levels of the physically handicapped pupils in the nine schools examined, given the severe restrictions of many of the handicapping conditions, can be described as favourable when compared with the attainment and achievement levels of their non-handicapped peers.

Teachers gave an overall assessment of ability, and rated 14 physically handicapped children as above average, 18 as about average and eight as a little below average (Table 8.1). The graphs in respect of the standardized scores of the *Neale Analysis of*

Reading Ability and the National Foundation for Educational Research *Basic Mathematical Tests*, show the levels of attainment and achievement of the Sample Group of physically handicapped children in relation to the two Control Groups of above average and below average ability, such groups being formed from class teachers' estimates based on classroom performance. It is encouraging to note the position of the physically handicapped pupils, and the results represented in graph form suggest their levels of attainment and achievement are higher than findings of earlier studies. In just four cases, the child's progress was so slow and his difficulties such that transfer to a special school had been arranged, in view of the combination of learning problems and multiple physical handicaps, which made placement in a mainstream class unrealistic. These pupils required additional resources and specialist support on a greater scale than was currently being provided.

The findings suggest a number of interesting results. First, most of the physically handicapped pupils in the Sample Group were well able to cope with, and to benefit from, the normal curriculum of a mainstream school. Secondly, in the main, this included the majority of those handicapped pupils with associated learning difficulties and neurological abnormalities, and this factor signifies some change in the kind of special educational needs which are now being met by programmes of integration. The four pupils being transferred to special schools were all neurologically handicapped, however, and this accentuates the need for better financial support to provide additional resources and specialist facilities.

Perceptions amongst pupils

The favourable endorsement of the integration programme in their school by the staff has been noted, and non-handicapped pupils accepted peers with special needs, albeit in various degrees, in to the membership of the school community. So, attitudes towards pupils with special needs were generally positive. The handicapped pupils' age and capacity for communication were the two prominent factors which appeared to influence the formation and evolution of attitudes, and the findings suggest that these factors have major relevance, where non-handicapped peers are concerned.

The lack of behavioural problems amongst pupils with special needs was stressed, and in many cases it was noted that the pupils' level of social maturity had been measurably heightened during the first year of integrated provision. Opportunities for social contact with non-handicapped peers were many and varied, and the majority of pupils in the Sample Group had made friends with non-handicapped children. In the main, most of the handicapped pupils had a wide circle of friends, some being children who lived in their home localities and with whom they enjoyed a variety of recreational and leisure activities, out of school hours. It was suggested by both teachers and parents that the physically handicapped pupils were popular with their non-handicapped peers and, furthermore, were respected and well-liked for their individual personalities and interests.

The main conclusion to emerge from the involvement of the Sample Group of pupils with special needs in the various integration programmes examined was that there was little or no evidence to suggest that the group as a whole was ascribed a handicapped or deviant identity because of either the individuals within it, or the perceptions and attitudes of individuals outside it. Equally, there was no evidence to suggest that individual pupils were stereotyped through group membership. A recommendation leading from these findings is that consideration must be given to the size of the group of handicapped pupils, to ensure that it is proportionate in relation to the whole school population. Hence, its identity as a group will not be markedly significant.

10
The Impact of the Education Act 1981

Possible solutions

The background to the integration debate and the changing climate
of opinion towards the concept of integration lend support to the
view that there is a case for making parents active participants with
other professionals in the early development of their handicapped
child. From the point of view of the parents, there is evidence to
suggest that their confidence in the various professionals is
reasonably positive, and is increasing with understanding.

The findings of this study indicate very clearly that parents want
their children to be educated in mainstream schools. The nature and
quality of the education on offer is the major concern of the parents,
and such a concern is not always acknowledged by the professionals
associated with the care of the handicapped child, and his eventual
school placement. Before a decision is taken to place a child in
integrated provision there needs to be a thorough and detailed
assessment of his needs; a clear understanding of what the benefits of
such a placement are likely to be; where difficulties are likely to
arise; and the fullest involvement of parents in both the decision and
the reasons for it. Some parents seek a more active role in the
education of their child than others, but many schools appear to
enlist the co-operation of parents effectively, so they are allocated
tasks which are meaningful and designed to promote greater
co-operation between home and school. Contact between the two is
organized in various ways and so serves different functions.

Parents are all too aware of the need for specialist attention,
but a recommendation which emerges from the findings of this
investigation is that in order to achieve maximum benefit from

specialist attention, it must be provided in a context of normality where the handicapped child interacts socially, emotionally and educationally with his non-handicapped peers. Several parents indicated such 'normality' had helped them to accept their handicapped child. Acceptance of the child with special needs in this way helps parents to believe that their child has a contribution to make to society, and whilst integration does not remove the special needs, it does place such needs in perspective.

Three distinctive steps emerged from this study, as essential attributes for active parental involvement. First, parents must be made welcome by the school, and at ease in the company of the staff; secondly, they must be encouraged and led to believe they can make an important contribution to their children's education; and, thirdly, they must be assigned specific tasks to assist this education, which are fully understood by them, and which appear relevant to their children's needs. It is desirable for consultation of this kind to be arranged on a regular basis as the integration programme develops, so that any problems which do arise can be discussed and dealt with before they reach an acute stage.

Teachers in mainstream classes must work closely with teachers experienced in special education to ascertain the pupils' special educational, physical and social needs. This kind of preparation is particularly helpful when pupils with special needs are to be placed full-time in mainstream classes. Where a teacher expresses apprehension, it is advisable to place a pupil with special needs for a trial period. It is essential that physically handicapped pupils are placed in classes where the teacher is enthusiastic towards integration. Information from the nine schools indicated that preparation of staff was generally acknowledged to be important, and adequate preparation was determined as the reason for positive attitudes and acknowledged goodwill amongst staff.

The focus of the study was on what might be achieved at local level and the findings revealed clear implications for initial and early in-service training.

Essential elements in initial teacher training courses

At present some initial training courses include an element of training concerning pupils with special educational needs. The

Advisory Committee on the Supply and Education of Teachers (ACSET) in their Report *Teacher Training and Special Educational Needs* published in June 1984 suggest that students should be prepared:

i   to have sufficiently detailed awareness of children's development and progress in learning so as to be able to identify special educational needs as they first arise, at whatever age, and including in the range both very young children and older pupils.

ii to adapt teaching methods and materials across the curriculum to the needs of individual pupils.

iii to appreciate the importance of establishing good working relationships with parents and to know how to profit from their collaborative support, which is of particular value in the case of pupils with special educational needs.

iv to be familiar with the range of specialist services available to pupils and parents, both from within and from outside schools, to see the teacher as a member of a multi-professional team, and to be able to judge when specialist help is needed.

The Secretary of State's criteria for the approval of initial teacher training courses has already stimulated institutions to develop their courses along these lines, and consideration is also being given to the involvement of suitably qualified practising school teachers in initial teacher training courses, and as an aid to staff development programmes. It is clear that the heads of department and senior staff involved with teacher training should institute regional and national seminars, as well as conferences, to consider how initial training courses might meet the Secretary of State's criteria.

In-service provision

The ACSET Report draws attention to the fact that each LEA has its own organizational arrangements for meeting special educational needs. The service which each LEA provides should have certain essential features in order to meet fully the needs of pupils and students. The Report describes these essential features which include

> LEA advisers with advanced specialised knowledge who are equipped to provide in-service training and to work together with training institutions, LEA administrators and heads of schools and colleges who organise the service so as to meet the needs of the full ability range, and teachers equipped to take specific responsibility for special needs pupils, not to mention a teacher force which is generally aware of the part it has to play.

A range of training provision is required to include long and short, full-time and part-time courses. Such a range will enable each LEA to achieve its determined goals and provide the resources to identify priority groups for particular types of training, and to meet the groups' specific needs. ACSET further recommend that:

(i) The headteacher of every school needs to be able to assume or delegate responsibility for ensuring that the special educational needs of pupils are identified and suitable provision made to meet those needs. All courses of management training for heads and senior staff should therefore include elements concerned with special educational needs and the organisation of resources to meet those needs.

(ii) Each school should have access to a designated teacher who is capable of identifying and devising strategies to overcome the impediments to pupils' learning, who can consider the implications for the curriculum of that school arising from the presence of pupils with a range of special educational needs and who can organise additional help in ways which will give such pupils access to the full range of the curriculum...

LEAs should therefore employ specialist teachers who can provide expert advice and who 'have detailed knowledge of the spectrum of special educational needs'.

> .....In order to help teachers to meet special needs through curricular and other forms of support, the core element of in-service training should include knowledge of the physical,

cognitive, emotional and social development of children, the principles and practice of curriculum development and evaluation, and the working of educational and other support services. Teachers will also need practical strategies for matching provision to need, through adapting and extending the curriculum, collaborating with parents, other teachers and other professionals, and mobilizing the resources of the community.

Emphasis should be placed on improving teacher skills in the identification of *all* pupils' special needs, not simply the two per cent of the school population with severe and complex disabilities; in preparing individualized learning programmes rather than class teaching programmes and in using developmental sequenced learning strategies involving the mastering of learning techniques. Teachers need to be taught how to prepare and use monitoring and recording procedures, linked to pupils' learning and aimed at improving learning, and to be familiar with appropriate organization and methodology.

Components on handicap in initial training courses for all teachers should include more lectures, seminars, visits to schools, and, of particular importance, experience of actual informal contact with handicapped children. Well thought out and extended teacher training is an essential prerequisite to guide staff into integrated provision, and to establish a career structure. Findings stress the critical need for such training if the principle of integration is to gain momentum. Very few teachers in the survey group, just nine in all, had undertaken courses of specialist training in aspects of special educational provision. Only a small number had taken one or more short courses relating to special needs. Whilst it would be both inappropriate and impractical to ratify the deficiencies of initial training, or provide a substitute for formal full-time or part-time in-service courses, further adaption of and supplementation of such courses are possible.

Participants in training courses need to share the knowledge gained with other colleagues and professionals from specialist agencies, in the form of 'custom built' local courses. From such local courses, staff of individual schools could develop a programme of integration appropriate to the needs of their handicapped pupils. Different aspects of professional interaction offer a variety of training possibilities, through participating jointly in common professional tasks, sharing expertise, collaboration in the form of visits, review meetings and case conferences, and in team teaching and working together. Such training will influence further the opinions and perceptions of the teacher towards integration, resulting in a great many more teachers subscribing to the view that considerable benefits are gained by the handicapped and non-handicapped pupils alike, through placement in the mainstream.

Because many handicapped children have a multiplicity of special needs, there should be a designated person within the LEA who has overall responsibility for seeing that the recommendations of those different agencies relating to the placement of physically handicapped children within mainstream schools, are implemented. A suggestion is that this person could be the adviser for special education, with special responsibility for clearly defined groups of handicapped children within mainstream schools. At the organizational level, it should be quite clear who has the responsibility for planning and maintaining schemes of integrated provision. It is recommended that arrangements be made for the overall suitability of the placement to be reviewed each year and, in particular, the progress the child with special needs is making in integrating into the mainstream class, should be regularly reviewed to ensure that they are receiving the necessary support.

In all schools with provision for physically handicapped pupils, the school medical officer would be expected to play a central role. Some of the recommendations in the Court Report (1976) are highly relevant, in particular one which stresses the value of a medical assessment of every child before he goes to school full-time, following which 'teachers should learn directly from the doctor and nurse, about conditions which require their informed response and understanding. In this way they would acquire greater insight into the pupils in their charge and feel more secure and adequate in teaching those with special needs'. All schools with integrated provision for groups of physically handicapped children would benefit from having a member of staff with nursing qualifications and appropriate training. Many physically handicapped pupils of primary age need regular therapy, and physiotherapy and speech therapy should be provided on the school premises.

Where adequate therapy provision is available, the service is quite successful, and members of the ancillary staff are able to follow routine exercises with the pupils under the therapists' direction. A problem which frequently arises, however, is the lack of time available for consultation between school staff and personnel from specialist agencies. A time for consultative meetings needs to be set aside, and internal case conferences and placement reviews involving external specialists as and when available would be particularly welcome.

LEAs do need to consider setting up carefully planned and adequately funded programmes of integration in selected primary schools with a view to fully meeting the special educational needs of pupils. Whatever form integrated provision takes, it is not unreasonable to expect LEAs to put as much in the way of resources as has previously been put into special schools. The form which special provision takes is a reflection of policy. The quality of the provision is not. Rather, it reflects the resources put into it and the level of supportive services.

There are many children in the severely physically handicapped groups whose ability to learn is initially, at least, probably no different from that of an average child. Too many of these children, even the most intelligent, become educationally backward and emotionally disturbed, not as a direct result of their handicap, but as a consequence of the interference it causes with normal development and schooling. Therefore a major factor in planning help is the level of the child's learning ability. The greater the degree of handicap the higher must be the child's general level of ability in order to overcome the obstacles which his disability imposes on his educational development (Wall, 1979).

Implications for the future

The concept of integration is an educational controversy which has drawn attention to the ways in which educational policies evolve. The movement to integrate children with special educational needs in mainstream schools is firmly founded, and the principle is here to stay. Integration is now a fact of educational life in the disabled community.

The real questions now are not so much 'whether and why' but 'how, when and where and for whom' integration:

(a) Does the expansion of integration, backed by positive commitment, carry within itself the seeds of a new major inequality?
(b) Will integrated pupils with special needs become the 'haves', those still in special schools the 'have nots'?
(c) Is there a need to develop a unified system, interrelating integrated schemes and special schools, with extensive and easy transfer between the two?
(d) Will there be little to gain from letting special schools decay, but much to gain from their acquiring new responsibilities?

However, even amongst the advocates of integrated education, there is doubt that integration is suitable for every child with special needs, and no country has relinquished its special schools altogether. There will always be a large group of severely multipli-handicapped children for whom integrated education would offer little or no benefit. There are many borderline cases, where a procedure which envelops a comprehensive education and assessment of individual needs can have positive and potential benefits. The unsuitability and inappropriateness of integration arrangements can result in failed educational provision and restrict the opinions of those who seek to advocate integration.

The Fish Report which comes from an independent review committee, chaired by ex-HMI John Fish, on provision by ILEA to meet special educational needs confirms that decisions about special educational needs influence decisions about *all* educational needs. The educational rights of children and young people with special educational needs are seen as part of a single commitment to developing equal opportunities for all pupils within a comprehensive system. The Fish Report upholds the basic principle that the process of integration should form an essential element in *all* education whenever it takes place.

In order to break down the barriers between different kinds of institutions the Report recommends extending the idea of 'clusters' of neighbouring primary schools to enable them to work together to develop mutually supportive arrangements to meet special educational needs and provide a focus for the development of support services. The aim would be to facilitate the sharing of professional responsibilities in order to plan for a child's educational career as a whole, to explore possibilities for delivering specialist services to the mainstream setting and to encourage more active parental involvement.

To make this collaboration possible, it is necessary for a variety of professionals to accept common aims and understand each other's concerns and contributions. Joint planning and interprofessional training are vital, as special educational needs are relative rather than fixed as permanent attributes of individuals. 'They are relative to the ability of schools and colleges to meet the range of individual needs of the children and young people who attend them. This approach involves all teachers in understanding how special educational needs may arise and how their work may influence whether they arise or not.'

Equally essential is the provision of adequate resources. The Report suggests that resources released by changes in special school provision might be devoted to building up services in mainstream schools and colleges and supporting individuals with special educational needs in them. The re-allocation of resources is important as staff from special schools could be redeployed and their expertise used constructively in the development of integration. The aim is to involve those at present working in special schools in a stimulating and constructive way in the development of a more integrated system so that the quality of education and special educational provision can be built on. An evolutionary project aimed positively at an increase in opportunities and social interaction and a change in policy towards working more closely with teachers in mainstream schools. The Fish Report is the framework for an imaginative responsive and genuinely comprehensive education system.

The concentration given to such an educational controversy stresses the supreme importance of considering each child's educational needs independently and thinking of support and resources in a more flexible way. The study has highlighted the factors which are crucial if successful integration is to take place. Teachers need to be fully acquainted with the extent of their pupils' disabilities, if the pupils' insecurity and subsequent failure to adjust is to be overcome. They must be aware of the need for a tremendous amount of preparation, and an enormous degree of support from both special schools and from support services must be readily available.

Successful integration is dependent upon the involvement of parents from the moment their child's handicap is discovered. This is a critical time and adequate help at all levels must be made available to the family. The Education Act 1981 allows parents specific rights in the decision regarding placement, and once a child is placed in a mainstream school, regular communication between the parents, school and staff must be established and maintained.

There are two major factors which, therefore, must be given maximum consideration in future plans for integrated provision. First, the concept of special educational needs extends beyond consideration of specific handicap, and takes account of the total situation of the pupils as it affects their education. Second, as well as pupils who have permanent special educational needs, there are other pupils who will have special educational needs at some point in their school life, albeit on a temporary basis. The Education Act 1981 lacks the precision of the Warnock Report, and places its main emphasis on provision for children whose special education is the subject of a statement by the LEA. Consequently the Act fails to stress the importance of preventative special education within the mainstream school, and of the needs of the larger number of children who require proportionate special provision. This, in itself, poses enormous problems for mainstream schools who may already be attempting to meet the unacknowledged special needs of a large percentage of its pupils.

Hence the amount of resources in terms of staffing and specialized equipment for the more severely handicapped may be already stretched to the limit. Furthermore, the Act empowers the Secretary of State to make regulations governing the recognition of special schools, but does nothing to recognize the basic facilities which must essentially be made available in mainstream schools, for them to provide education for the children who are the subject of a statement of special educational needs. The omissions could well lead to ill-conceived attempts at 'integration on the cheap' as an alternative to special schools. The staff have a distinct role to promote clear and effective communication between all concerned with the development and educational placement of handicapped children and need to be aware of the extent of and availability of supportive services from specialist agencies. They must also familiarize themselves with what resources are available from the LEA in terms of specialist equipment for use in the classroom and school situation.

The mainstream school must make available to its physically handicapped pupils a sufficient proportion of the physical, social and educational activities of the school in order that they can participate on equal terms with their non-handicapped peers. This will afford opportunity for the realization of full potential and personal achievements, which will allow pupils with special educational needs to become fully accepted members of the mainstream school community, and a real part of the community in which they will live. In essence, effective integration.

Appendix A

Pupil Profiles: The Sample Group of Physically Handicapped Pupils

First School Age Pupils: 4.04 to 8.00 years. Mean Age: 5.95 years

Pupil	Age	Handicap	Neale Analysis of Reading Ability			NFER Mathematics Tests		Inferences
			Rate	Accuracy	Comprehension	Score	Test	
1	6.00	Cerebral Palsy	No score –		Below recommended age range for testing purposes.			
2	4.10	Spina Bifida	No score –		Below recommended age range for testing purposes.			
3	5.00	Muscular Atrophy	No score –		Below recommended age range for testing purposes.			
4	6.06	Siamese Twin	6.03	6.09	6.03	73	A	Note this child was able to attempt the tests although not in the recommended age range.
5	6.05	Cerebral Palsy	No score –		Below recommended age range for testing purposes.			
6	4.11	Spina Bifida	No score –		Below recommended age range for testing purposes.			
7	4.07	Muscular Atrophy	No score –		Below recommended age range for testing purposes.			
8	6.08	Rheumatoid Arthritis	No score –		Below recommended age range for testing purposes.			

						Score		Comments
9	6.09	Brain Damage (Accident)	6.06	8.04	8.08	95	A	Low reading rate score, due to severe accident damage which affected speech.
10	7.02	Cerebral Palsy	7.02	7.03	7.04	104	A	
11	7.10	Brain Damage (Birth)	9.01	9.05	9.05	99	A	
12	6.10	Spina Bifida	7.06	8.03	8.03	114	A	
13	6.00	Haemophilia	6.06	7.00	7.03	103	A	Note this child was able to attempt the tests, although below the recommended age range.
14	7.05	Lower Limb Paralysis	9.00	9.03	10.11	116	A	
15	7.00	Rheumatoid Arthritis	No score –		Unable to attempt tests because of severe emotional and behavioural problems.			
16	6.08	Haemophilia	6.08	7.09	7.10	103	A	A hesitant reader.
17	5.05	Spina Bifida	No score –		Below recommended age range for testing purposes			
18	6.11	Spina Bifida	9.00	11.06	11.04	105	A	Excellent ability in reading skills. Average attainment in mathematical skills in common with handicapping condition.
19	7.06	Cerebral Palsy	8.06	11.09	12.00	133	A	Reading rate score lower than other scores, due to severe speech impediment associated with handicap.

Sample Group of Physically Handicapped Children Middle School Age Pupils: 7.07 to 12.06 years. Mean Age: 9.11 years

Pupil	Age	Handicap	Neale Analysis of Reading Ability			NFER Mathematics Tests		Inferences
			Rate	*Accuracy*	*Comprehension*	*Score*	*Test*	
1	12.01	Muscular Dystrophy	10.03	11.06	11.08	91	C	
2	9.07	Muscular Atrophy	11.04	11.01	12.06	126	C	
3	11.03	Spina Bifida	12+	11.11	11.10	112	DE	An encouraging score in reading ability, given that this child speaks English as his second language.
4	11.05	Cerebral Palsy	9.04	11.08	12.01	117	DE	Note the low reading rate score. This might be attributed to a speech impediment associated with handicap.
5	10.01	Spina Bifida	11.10	11.09	11.06	125	C	
6	11.01	Cerebral Palsy	10.05	11.11	11.08	116	DE	Note the lower reading rate score. This might be attributed to the fact that the child is multi-ethnic, and has a speech difficulty associated with handicap.
7	9.07	Cerebral Palsy	9.07	11.09	11.10	133	C	It might be suggested that spasticity of the throat muscles causes this child to read laboriously.
8	9.08	Polio	8.09	9.02	7.06	96	B	Limited progress in both tests, attributed to English as a second language.

								Comments
9	9.02	Muscular Atrophy	10.03	11.08	11.06	126	B	
10	8.06	Spina Bifida	8.09	11.01	11.02	126	B	
11	7.11	Rubella Syndrome	13+	11.08	11.10	101	A	The scores suggest excellent reading skills, the acquiring of which might well be attributed to a gross lack of mobility.
12	8.06	Muscular Dystrophy	8.09	9.01	8.08	90	B	
13	10.02	Muscular Dystrophy	10.10	11.05	11.01	98	C	
14	9.09	Hemiplegia	10.04	11.11	11.01	121	C	
15	8.00	Heart Defect	10.04	9.03	9.06	115	A	
16	9.00	Spina Bifida	6.07	11.08	11.10	120	B	Low score in reading rate due perhaps to initial nervousness and lack of confidence.
17	10.02	Cerebral Palsy	11.00	11.07	11.10	121	C	
18	11.05	Spina Bifida	11.00	12.01	12.05	114	DE	
19	11.09	Brain Damage (Accident)	No scores	–	Unable to attempt tests due to severe limitations of handicap.			

Pupil	Age	Handicap	Neale Analysis of Reading Ability			NFER Mathematics Tests		Inferences
			Rate	Accuracy	Comprehension	Score	Test	
20	9.10	Brain Damage (Birth)	8.03	9.00	9.05	70	B	This child has difficulty in mastering the various mathematical concepts.
21	9.04	Brain Damage (Accident)	8.02	8.10	8.07	124	B	Poor concentration span and memory recall caused by handicap. A high score in the maths test indicates the ability to master concrete operations.
22	9.08	Arthrogryposis	8.08	11.02	11.02	114	C	
23	9.01	Imperforate Anus	9.03	10.01	11.01	127	B	Lacks confidence in reading, resulting in low reading rate, because of emotional insecurity associated with handicap.
24	8.11	Arthrogryposis	10.03	12.01	12.09	124	B	
25	9.04	Muscular Atrophy	8.06	9.04	9.03	121	B	
26	8.03	Spina Bifida	7.08	7.07	7.03	71	B	Some indication of learning disabilities, frequently associated with handicap.
27	8.07	Imperforate Anus	8.05	8.10	9.01	115	B	
28	8.02	Spina Bifida	8.10	10.90	11.10	128	A	An unusually high score in maths for a pupil with Spina Bifida.
29	8.11	Brittle Bones	8.09	8.10	9.03	112	B	
30	7.09	Cerebral Palsy	No scores. Unable to attempt due to severe limitations imposed by handicaps.					
31	7.09	Familial Rickets	7.10	11.03	10.11	114	A	Reads methodically and slowly, with great care and interest.

Appendix B

Section A: The setting up of the integration programme

1. Who proposed integrating physically handicapped children in the school?
2. When did the integration programme begin?
3a. Did the school building have to be adapted?
3b. Is so, how, and to what extent?
4a. Were the opinions of the staff sought, before integration began?
4b. Did staff choose to have handicapped pupils in their classes?
5. How were the staff prepared beforehand?
    (a) Did they visit special schools?
    (b) Where did they gain information about the various physical handicaps, and from whom?
    (c) Did they meet the handicapped child prior to admission?
    (d) Did they receive adequate information about the children beforehand?
6. In what type of school were the handicapped children placed before?

Section B: The handicapped pupils

1. How many handicapped pupils in the school at present?
2. Could more handicapped children be catered for? If no, why not?
3. How many classes have handicapped pupils? What is the class size?

4. What is the range of physical handicap?
5. What is the age range?
6. What is the ability range?
7. What is the criteria for the admission of handicapped pupils?
8. How are the handicapped pupils assessed prior to admission and by whom?
   (a) academic assessment
   (b) medical assessment
9. Do the handicapped pupils visit the school prior to admission? If so, how much time do they spend, and are any accepted on a trial period basis?
10. Are there any aspects of the curriculum that the handicapped pupil cannot participate in?
11. What are the major benefits of integrated education?
12. What problems and difficulties have been encountered?
13. What do you do if the handicapped pupil is underachieving? Is specialist and remedial help available?
14a. How do the pupils mix socially?
14b. What are the opportunities (i) inter classroom, (ii) out of school?
15. What areas of difficulty present problems for the handicapped pupil?
    (a) mobility   (f) communication
    (b) access   (g) need for specialist equipment
    (c) toileting   (h) teasing/bullying
    (d) transport   (i) other problems
    (e) recording

Section C: Staff

1a. How many staff are involved in the integration programme?
1b. Do they have appropriate responsibility posts?
1c. Do they receive a responsibility allowance?
2. Are the staff concerned specially qualified and/or experienced? Is there in-service training provision?
   (a) in school
   (b) in LEA
3a. How many ancillary staff are employed? Is this number adequate? What are their specific duties?

3b. Qualifications of ancillary staff? Would they like to have specific additional training?

4. How many therapists are involved? Full-time or part-time?

5. Have you adequate equipment and resources?

6. What kind of support do you have from?
(a) headteacher   (b) other colleagues
(c) physiotherapists   (d) speech therapists
(e) educational psychologists (f) special schools adviser
(g) school medical officer/hospitals/clinics
(h) social services   (i) parents
(j) local education authority (k) welfare officer
(l) health visitor
Is the support adequate? If not, why not?

7. Are case conferences held? How often? Who is involved?

8. Have you encountered any specific problems?

9. Are you in favour of integration? Do you feel it is working in the handicapped pupils' best interests?

10. What are the aims for your handicapped pupils?

11. What are the non-handicapped pupils' attitudes towards the handicapped? Are they taught about handicaps? How are attitudes revealed in behaviour?

12. What do these children gain from having handicapped pupils in their class? Are there any disadvantages or restrictions?

Appendix C

Questionnaire for Class Teacher

Name of child: School:
Date of birth: Form: No. in form:
Nature of handicap: District:

Section A: Extent and effect of physical disability

1. *Transport*
   (i) How does the child get to school – does he require special transport? Please specify and give details.
   (ii) Does anyone usually accompany the child to and from school?
   (iii) Are there any problems over getting to school?

2. *Mobility*
   (i) Is the child able to walk and run as well as a normal child of this age?
   (ii) Does the child have any physiotherapy? If so, please specify and give details.
   (iii) Is the child's gait abnormal at all? Please specify and give details.
   (iv) Does the child wear or use any mechanical aids to mobility, e.g. calipers, elbow crutches, special boots? If yes, does the child ever need a wheelchair in school? Please specify and give details.
   (v) Does the child have difficulty in walking long distances or with stairs? Please specify and give details.

(vi) Can you name any activities in which the child is impeded by poor mobility, or excluded altogether? If so, do the other children make allowances or offer to help in any way? Please specify and give details.

3. *Manipulative ability*
   (i) Does the child have any disability or weakness of the upper limbs or hand? If so, please specify and give details.
   (ii) Does the child have any difficulty in carrying out the following tasks? Please tick as appropriate.

   writing   using a rubber   using scissors
   drawing   ruling lines   craft activities
   steadying paper for writing
   opening desk and removing book
   opening book or turning the pages
   handling other education equipment
   other manipulation: handles, switches, etc.

   (iii) If the child has difficulties of this kind, do the other children offer help spontaneously? Please specify and give details.
   (iv) Is there anything on the curriculum from which the child is excluded because of such difficulties? Please specify and give details.
   (v) What sort of allowance do you make for the child under the circumstances? e.g. testing, marking, handwriting, etc.

4. *Self-care*
   Toilet
   (i) Is the child sometimes incontinent of the bladder or bowels in school?
   (ii) If so, does the child wear a urinal or ileostomy bag?
   (iii) How much help does he need in going to the toilet, and if help is required, who supplies it? Please specify and give details.

   Feeding
   Does the child require any special assistance at meals, and if so, who helps him?

Dressing
(i) Does the child require help with dressing?
(ii) If yes, please tick those where help is required:

Socks and/or shoes   Fastenings
Clothes, upper part of body   Appliances (calipers, etc.)
Clothes, lower part of body

5. *Hearing*
   (i) Do you think that the child's hearing is normal?
   (ii) Does the child wear a hearing aid?
   (iii) If an aid is worn, is the child's hearing good, moderate, poor?

6. *Speech*
   (i) Is the child's speech normal for someone of this age?Please specify and give details.
   (ii) If speech is at all defective, do you think therapy is required?
   (iii) If therapy is provided, where does it take place?

7. *Sight*
   (i) Does the child wear glasses?
   (ii) If no, do you think the child's sight is defective?
   (iii) If glasses are worn, do these correct the child's vision?

8. Does the child have any other physical difficulties relating to his handicap which have not been mentioned? Please specify and give details if necessary.

9. *Special aids*
   (i) Furniture – does the child require any special furniture, or modification to existing furniture? If so, please specify and give details.
   (ii) Equipment – does the child have any special equipment? (e.g. pencils, bag, typewriter, feeding utensils, etc.) If so, please specify and give details.
   (iii) Buildings, etc. – have any other modifications been made in the school for the child's benefit? Please specify and give details.

(iv) Suggestions – is there any special equipment or modification which you think would be helpful for the child? Please specify and give details.

Section B: Academic

10. Has your child been selected by streaming? Please specify and give details.

11. *Extra help*
Do you think the child would benefit from extra help in anything, and if so, is he actually getting it? Please specify and give details.

12. *General assessment*
    (i) How do you feel the child is getting on generally in his schoolwork compared with others in the class? Please specify and give details.
    (ii) If the child is below average, do you feel that he ever uses his handicap as an excuse to be lazy?

Section C: Social

13. Do you think that the child is popular, and are there any special friends?

14.
    (i) Does the child ever get teased and is there much teasing in the school as a whole?
    (ii) If so, how does it come to your attention?
    (iii) How often does the child get teased, and for what reason?
    (iv) How does the child react to teasing?
    (v) How do you generally cope with teasing, and have you discovered any particularly effective way of so doing?
    (vi) Apart from teasing, do the other children show much curiosity about the child's handicap? If so, what is the child's reaction to this?
    (vii) Do you think that the child gets bullied more than the other children?

15. Does the child play much with other children in the playground? If so, is it usually in a group or with one or two individuals?

16. Are there any group activities which the child's handicap excludes him from? Please specify.

17. Does the child have any particular class duties?

Section D: Teacher's management of the handicapped child

18.
  (i)   Did you know you were going to have a handicapped child in your class beforehand, and if so, how did you know?
  (ii) Did you know the nature of the child's handicap and did it worry you at all? If worried, in what respect?

19. Do you know any other physically handicapped people?

20.
  (i)   Did anyone give you any information about this particular child, and if so, from what source, or sources, was the information received to help you understand the child and any relevant problems? Please specify and give details.
  (ii) Was any information you received satisfactory or do you feel there could have been more which would have enabled you to understand this child's problems better?

21. If you were worried about having the child in your class originally, what are your reactions now? Please specify.

22.
  (i)   Have you on any occasion talked to the other children as a group about the child's handicap? If so, how and why was this done? Please specify and give details.
  (ii) Do you feel you have to spend too much time helping the child at the expense of the other children?
  (iii) Are there any other problems which the child's presence in the class gives rise to? Please specify and give details.

23.

    (i) Have you met either of the child's parents, or another close relative, and if so, can you remember what you discussed with them? Please give details.

    (ii) What impression did you get of the mother's (or mother substitute's) attitude to the handicap?

Section E: Placement

24.

    (i) Do you think this is the best type of school for the child to be in at present, and if not, where do you think he would be better placed? Please specify.

    (ii) Do you think the child will manage to cope with an ordinary secondary school?

Thank you very much for your help. I am grateful to you for giving up so much time to answer this questionnaire.

This questionnaire was compiled with assistance from Dr E. M. Anderson.

Appendix D

Questionnaire for Families

Section A: Family background

1. *Children*
   (i) How many children in your family?
   (ii) What position in your family is your handicapped child? i.e.
        third, second, first
   (iii) Are any of your other children handicapped? If so, please
        specify.

2.
   (i) Have you made any special permanent arrangements or
        adaptations in the house/flat for your handicapped child? If
        so, please give details.
   (ii) Are there any/any other special adaptations which you
        really *need* for your handicapped child? If so, please give
        details.

Section B: Physical handicap

3. *Mobility*
   (i) Does your child have any abnormality/problems at all
        affecting his/her legs and mobility? If so, please give details.
   (ii) How much difficulty does he/she have in getting around
        inside the home? e.g. from room to room, stairs. Please give
        details.

(iii) Does he/she use any special aids for getting around? YES/NO
Please tick those appropriate.

special boots/shoes   wheelchair less than half the time
a stick   wheelchair more than half the time
calipers   other
crutches   not applicable

4. When going out, for instance to visit friends within walking distance, can your child manage on his/her own or does he/she need assistance? Please give details.

5. *Public transport*
    Has your child ever been anywhere by bus, train or underground? Please give details of any journey undertaken and any difficulties encountered.

6. *Usual method of transport*
    When your child wants to go out somewhere not within easy walking distance, what is his/her *usual* means of getting there? Please specify and give details.

7. *Hand control*
    Does your child have any difficulties? If so, please specify and give details.

8. *Upper limb impairment*
    (i) Does your child use any special aids at school to help with this problem? If so, please specify and give details.
    (ii) Does your child use any special aids at home? Please specify and give details.

9. *Toileting*
    Does your child need any assistance with toileting? If so, please give details.

10.
    Has your child a toileting problem?

11.

Do you feel this problem is affecting your child's relationship with other children of his/her age in any way? If so, please give details.

12.

How does your child feel about the toileting problem?

13. *Penile appliance*
    (i) If your child has a penile appliance, do you feel this way of coping is satisfactory? If not, in what way is it unsatisfactory?
    (ii) How does your child feel about this way of coping?

14.

If your child wears an appliance of any kind, how does he/she cope with it? Completely alone? Or is some help required, for instance, when changing it?

15. *For those with appliances*
    Has your child ever been teased at school on account of wearing an appliance? If so, please give details.

16. *Speech*
    (i) Does your child have any difficulties with speech? If so, please specify and give details. To what extent do other people have any difficulty in understanding your child? Please detail.
    (ii) If there is a speech defect, has your child ever had speech therapy? If so, is he/she still having it? Please specify and give details.

17.
    (i) Do you think your child's speech difficulties have made it more difficult for him/her to make friends than other children? If so, please specify and give details of how and when this has occurred.
    (ii) If it has affected friendships, do you think your child's speech difficulties have had a greater effect on his/her other relationships with other children at primary school? If so, please specify.

Section C: Schooling

18.

For how many years has your child been at his/her present school?

19. *Transport/distance*
(i) How does your child usually get to school?
(ii) How long does the journey to school usually take?

20.
(i) What type of school does your child attend and how do you feel about his/her going there? Do you feel that on the whole it's the right kind of school for him/her?
(ii) Has the school met your expectations? If not, please specify and give details.

21.
(i) As far as you know, is your child happy at this school? If not, do you know why he/she is not (entirely) happy at school? Please specify and give details.
(ii) Would you say that your child was happier at his/her special school, or have you not really noticed any difference? If any difference, please specify and give details.

22.

How well is your child getting on with his/her school work compared with other boys and girls of his/her age? As far as you know, is he/she (please tick as appropriate)?

Above average   A bit below average
About average   Making slow progress
Don't know

23.

Do you think your child worries about his/her work? If so, in what way, and how do you cope with it?

24.

As far as you know, is you child's behaviour at school satisfactory, or are there problems? If so, please specify and give details.

25.

Have you been to see any of the teachers at your child's school over the past year? If yes, what was the purpose of your visit?

Section D: Peer relationships

26.

How well does your child get on with other boys and girls of his/her own age? Does he/she mix fairly easily or are there problems? If so, please specify and give details.

27.

Does your child like company or does he/she prefer to do things on his/her own?

28.

(i)   Does your child have any friends his/her own age whom he/she sees outside school? Please give details.
(ii) If there are friends, are they quite a bit older or younger, or are they around the same age? Please give details.

29.

Does your child have as many friends now as when he/she was at special school? Please give details, if appropriate.

30.

(i)   Does your child know any other children with handicaps? If so, are any of them friends?
(ii) Does your child have any real friends with handicaps?
(iii) If yes to either of the preceding questions, would you say that most of your child's friends are physically handicapped, non-handicapped, or a mixture?

31.

Do your child's friends ever come round to your home to see him/her? How many times during a week in the holidays would friends be likely to come round to see your child? Please specify and give details.

32.

Does your child go to the homes of his/her friends? How often during a week in the holidays? Please specify and give details.

33.

Does your child ever go out with a group of friends (apart from clubs, etc.)? If so, please specify numbers, ages, sex, how regularly and what sort of things they do.

34.

   (i) Do you think your child has as many friends as boys and girls of his/her age who are not handicapped?

   (ii) If not, what do you feel are the *main* reason(s) for this?

35.

Does your child ever feel lonely? If so, how do you know? Does it happen at any particular time? How often? Please specify and give details.

Section E: Child's relationship with family

36. *If applicable*
   (i) Does your child spend much time with his/ her brother(s)/ sister(s) when he/she is not at school? Please specify and give details.
   (ii) How well do they get on together? About the same as most children, or better? Do they quarrel and get on each other's nerves quite frequently? If so, how and why? Please specify and give details.

37. *Mothers*
How well does your child get on with you? Do you disagree or quarrel at all? If so, when and why?

38.

    (i) During the last year, has your child ever talked to you about his/her handicap? If so, when and why, etc? If not, why? Please specify and give details.

    (ii) If yes, do you find you can talk to your child quite easily about his/her handicap, or do you find this rather difficult to do? What about your child?

39.

How does your child get on with your husband? Do they quarrel or get on each other's nerves much? If so, why and when?

40.

    (i) Does your child discuss his/her handicap with his/her father? If so, when and why?

    (ii) If yes, is the subject discussed with difficulty or not? What about your child?

41.

Would you say that your child finds it easier to discuss his/her handicap with you or his/her father, or is there no difference?

42.

Apart from you (and your husband) is there anyone else in whom your child really confides about his/her handicap? If so, who? Please specify and give details.

43.

Is your child usually happy, or is he/she quite often miserable? If unhappy, please specify how, when, why, etc.

44.

Has your child ever said that everything seems hopeless and nothing is worthwhile? If so, please specify and give details.

45.

    (i) If there is a problem of misery/depression, have you found anything you can say or do to help your child cope when he/she is feeling really low? If so, please specify and give details.

(ii) Is there anything which your child does which helps him/her to cope with any feelings of misery/ depression? If so, please specify and give details.

46.

Does your child ever have moods of being cross or irritable, or temper tantrums? If so, please specify and give details.

Thank you very much for your help. I am grateful to you for giving up so much time to answer this questionnaire.

This questionnaire was compiled with assistance from Dr E. M. Anderson.

Appendix E

Developmental Checklist: School C

Name: ....
Date of Birth: ....

	Autumn			Spring			Summer		
	Has diff.	Above ave.	Comment	Has diff.	Above ave.	Comment	Has diff.	Above ave.	Comment

Physical
1. Eyesight ....
2. Hearing ....
3. Speech ....
4. Hand–eye co-ordination ....
5. General bodily control ....

Social: Emotional and intellectual development
1. Plays alone ....
2. Plays alongside others ....
3. Plays with others ....
4. Leads in play ....
5. Ability to make relationships with peers ....
6. Ability to make relationships with adults ....
7. Receptive to change ....
8. Appears to be happy and settled in school situation ....
9. General awareness of environment .....
10. Ability to play imaginatively ....
11. Ability to play constructively ....
12. Ability to play purposefully ....
13. Ability to choose a task ....
14. Ability to persist at a task ....
15. Ability to create recognizable objects ....
16. Ability to make himself understood .....
17. Ability to listen with understanding .....
18. Ability to hold a simple conversation ...
19. Ability to talk about experiences ....
20. Attempts to describe and discuss his environment ....
21. Visual discrimination ....
22. Auditory discrimination ....
23. Tactile discrimination ....

References

AINSCOW, M. and TWEDDLE, D.A. (1979). *Preventing Classroom Failure*. Chichester: John Wiley and Sons.

ANDERSON, E.M. (1973). *The Disabled Schoolchild*. London: Methuen.

ARGYLE, M. (1972). *The Psychology of Interpersonal Behaviour*. London: Penguin Books.

ASPIN, D.N. (1982). 'Towards a concept of human being as a basis for a philosophy of special education', *Education Review*, 34, 2.

BAILEY, T. (1981). 'How can a headteacher make his special school special?' Appendix: *Journal of British Institute of Mental Handicap*, 9, 2.

BAKER, J.L. and GOTTLIEB, J. (1980). 'Attitudes of teachers towards mainstreaming retarded children'. In: GOTTLIEB, J. (Ed) *Educating Mentally Retarded Persons in the Mainstream*. Baltimore: University Park Press.

BAREN, M., LIEBL, R. and SMITH, L. (1978). *Overcoming Learning Difficulties: A Team Approach*. Keston, Virginia 22090, USA: Keston Publishing Company.

BARKER LUNN, J. (1966). *Primary Children's Attitude Scales*. Slough: NFER.

BARTON, L. and TOMLINSON, S. (1981). *Special Education: Policy, Practices and Social Issues*. London: Harper and Row.

BOLAM, R., SMITH, G. and CANTER, H. (1978). *LEA Advisers and the Mechanism of Innovation*. Slough: NFER.

BRENNAN, W.K. (1982a). *Changing Special Education*. Milton Keynes: Open University Press.

BRENNAN, W.K. (1982b). *Special Education in Mainstream Schools:*

The Search for Quality. Stratford-upon-Avon: National Council for Special Education.

BRITTON, E. (1978). 'Warnock and integration', *Educational Research*, 21, 1, 3 – 9.

BURDEN, R. (1978) 'Schools system analysis'. In: GILHAM, W. *Reconstructing Educational Psychology*. London: Croom Helm.

CANFIELD, J. and WELLS, H.C. (1976). *100 Ways to Enhance Self-Concept in the Classroom*. Hemel Hempstead: Prentice Hall International.

CANNON, J. (1975). Attitudes of teachers and fifth-year pupils in comprehensive schools towards pupils with physical disabilities. Unpublished Dip Ed thesis, University of Birmingham.

CARR, J., HALLIWELL, M.D. and PEARSON, A.M. (1983). 'Educational attainments of spina bifida children attending ordinary or special schools', *Special Education: Forward Trends*, 10, 3, 22 – 24, Research Supplement.

CHAZAN, M., LAING, A., SHACKLETON BAILEY, M. and JONES, G. (1980). *Some of Our Children*. Somerset: Open Books.

COPE, C. and ANDERSON, E. M. (1977). *Special Units in Ordinary Schools*. London: University of London, Institute of Education.

COURT REPORT. GREAT BRITAIN. DEPARTMENT OF HEALTH AND SOCIAL SECURITY. COMMITTEE ON CHILD HEALTH SERVICES (ENGLAND) (1976). *Fit for the Future*. London:HMSO.

CROLL, P., MOSES, D., WRIGHT, J. and BERNBAUM, G. (1982). The teacher's view of special educational needs in the junior classroom. University of Southampton. Paper prepared for the International Research and Development Seminar on Special Educational Needs.

CRUICKSHANK, S.M. (1981). *Concepts in Learning Disabilities*. New York: Syracuse University Press.

DOCKING, J.W. (1980). *Control and Discipline in Schools*. London: Harper and Row.

FISH, J. (1985). *Educational Opportunities For All*. Report of the John Fish Committee reviewing special educational provision. London: ILEA.

FOSTER, K.W. (1975). 'Physically handicapped children in an ordinary school'. In: LORING, J. and BURN, G. *Integration of Handicapped Children in Society*. London: Routledge and Kegan Paul.

GARNETT, J. (1976). 'Special children in a comprehensive', *Special*

Education: Forward Trends, 3, 1, 8 – 11.

GLIEDMAN, J. and ROTH, W. (1981). 'Parents and professionals'. In: SWANN, W. (Ed) *The Practice of Special Education*. Oxford: Blackwell/Open University Press.

GOTTLIEB, J., COHEN, L. and GOLDSTEIN, L. (1974). 'Social contact and personal adjustment as variables relating to attitudes toward educable mentally retarded children?', *Training School Bulletin*, 71, 9 – 16.

GOTTLIEB, J. and MANY, M. (1979). 'Special and regular education teachers' attitude toward mainstreaming'. In: GOTTLIEB, J. (Ed) (1980) *Educating Mentally Handicapped Persons in the Mainstream*. Baltimore: University Park Press.

GREAT BRITAIN. ADVISORY COMMITTEE ON THE SUPPLY AND EDUCATION OF TEACHERS (1984). *Teacher Training and Special Educational Needs*. Unpublished report.

GREAT BRITAIN. DEPARTMENT OF EDUCATION AND SCIENCE (1981). *The Education Act 1981: Special Educational Needs*. London: HMSO.

GREAT BRITAIN. DEPARTMENT OF EDUCATION AND SCIENCE (1982a). *Assessment and Statements of Special Educational Needs*. London: HMSO.

GREAT BRITAIN. DEPARTMENT OF EDUCATION AND SCIENCE (1982b). *Education Act 1981, Circular 8/82*. London: HMSO.

GREAT BRITAIN. DEPARTMENT OF EDUCATION AND SCIENCE (1983). *The Education (Special Educational Needs) Regulations*. London: HMSO.

GREAT BRITAIN. MINISTRY OF EDUCATION (1954). *Provision of Special Schools, Circular 176*. London: HMSO.

GULLIFORD, R. (1977). 'Trends in special education', *Education Review*, 29, 4, 233 – 240.

GURALNICK, M.J. (1978). 'Early classroom based intervention and the role of organisational structure', *Exceptional Children*, 42, 1, 25 – 31.

HALLIDAY, M.A.K. (1973). *Explorations in the Functions of Language*. London: Routledge and Kegan Paul.

HARDY, R.E. and CULL, J.G. (1974). *Severe Disabilities: Social and Rehabilitation Approaches*. Springfield, Illinois: Charles C. Thomas.

HASKELL, S.H. (1972). *Arithmetical Disabilities in Programmed Instruction: A Remedial Approach*. Springfield, Illinois:

Charles C. Thomas.

HEGARTY, S. and POCKLINGTON, K. (1981). *Educating Pupils with Special Needs in the Ordinary School.* Windsor: NFER-NELSON.

HEGARTY, S. and POCKLINGTON, K. (1982). *Integration in Action.* Windsor: NFER-NELSON.

HEWETT, F.H. (1976). *The Emotionally Disturbed Child in the Classroom.* London: Allyn and Bacon.

HEWETT, S. (1970). *The Family and the Handicapped Child.* London: Allen and Unwin.

HOWARTH, S.B. (1979). Changing patterns in the education of physically handicapped children. Unpublished Dip Ed thesis, University of London.

HOWARTH, S.B. (Ed) (1984). *The Head's Legal Guide.* New Malden: Croner Publications.

JAMIESON, M., PARLETT, M. and POCKLINGTON, K. (1977). *Towards Integration.* Windsor: NFER-NELSON.

JONES, E. (1980). The Carterton project. Unpublished M Ed thesis, University of Birmingham.

JONES, E. (1981). 'A resource approach to meeting special needs in a secondary school'. In: BARTON, L. and TOMLINSON, S. *Special Education: Policy, Practices and Social Issues.* London: Harper and Row.

LASLETT, R. (1979). 'Integrating the maladjusted child', *Special Education: Forward Trends,* 8, 3, 36 – 39.

LEACH, D.J. and RAYBOULD, E.C. (1977). *Learning and Behaviour Difficulties in School.* London: Open Books.

McCALL, C. (1983). *Classroom Grouping for Special Need.* Stratford-upon-Avon: National Council for Special Education.

McCONACHIE, H. (1982). 'Fathers, mothers, siblings and the family: How do they see themselves?' In: MITTLER, P. and McCONACHIE, H. *Approaches to Parental Involvement.* London: Croom Helm.

MEISGEIER, C. (1976). 'A review of critical issues indulging mainstreaming'. In: MANN, L. and SABATINO, D.A. (Eds) *The Third Review of Special Education.* Philadelphia: JSE Press.

MITTLER, P.J. (1972). 'Language and communication' University of Manchester, Hester Adrian Research Centre. In: CLARKE, A.M. and CLARKE, A.D.B. (Eds) (1974). *Mental Deficiency: The Changing Outlook.* London: Methuen.

MITTLER, P.J. (1979). *People not Patients: Problems and Policies in Mental Handicap.* London: Methuen.

MITTLER, P. and McCONACHIE, H. (1982). *Approaches to Parental Involvement*. London: Croom Helm.

MITTLER, P. and MITTLER, H. (1982). *Partnership with Parents*. Stratford-upon-Avon: National Council for Special Education.

MOSES, D. (1980). The assessment and incidence of special educational needs. A pilot study, University of Leicester.

NATIONAL FOUNDATION FOR EDUCATIONAL RESEARCH (1979). *Basic Mathematics Tests Series*. Windsor: NFER-NELSON.

NEALE, M.D. (1966). *Neale Analysis of Reading Ability*. London and Basingstoke: Macmillan Education.

PLOWDEN REPORT. GREAT BRITAIN. DEPARTMENT OF EDUCATION AND SCIENCE. CENTRAL ADVISORY COUNCIL FOR EDUCATION (ENGLAND) (1967). *Children and their Primary Schools*. London: HMSO.

POCKLINGTON, K. (1980). 'Integration – a lesson from America', *Special Education: Forward Trends*, 7, 3, 22 – 25.

PRINGLE, M.L.K. and FIDDES, D.O. (1970). *The Challenge of Thalidomide*. London: Longman.

REAY, D.G. (1979). 'Peer tutoring'. University of Newcastle, School of Education: *Newsletter No. 1*.

ROSE, C.D. (1979). The social interaction of severely mentally handicapped and normal children before and after a peer tutor programme. Unpublished thesis, University of Birmingham.

RUTTER, M., MAUGHAN, B., MORTIMER, P. and OUSTON, J. (1979). *Fifteen Thousand Hours*. London: Open Books.

SCHOOLS COUNCIL (1972). *Concept 7 – 9*. London: Longman.

SCHOOLS COUNCIL (1977). *Language for Learning*. London: Heinemann.

SHARP, J.D. and STOTT, D.H. (1976). *Effectiveness Motivation Scale* (Manual). Slough: NFER.

SMITH, B. (1982). 'Collaboration between parents and teachers of school age children'. In: MITTLER, P. and McCONACHIE, H. (1982) *Approaches to Parental Involvement*. London: Croom Helm.

TEW, B. and LAURENCE, K.M. (1972) 'The ability and attainments of spina bifida patients born in South Wales between 1952 and 1962', *Developmental Medicine and Child Neurology*, Supplement, 27, 124 – 131.

TEW, B. and LAURENCE, K.M. (1978). 'Differences in reading achievement between spina bifida children attending normal schools, and those attending special schools', *Child*, 4, 317 – 326.

THOMAS, D.N. (1975). 'The teacher and the handicapped child'. In: LORING, J. and BURN, G. *Integration of Handicapped Children in Society*. London: Routledge and Kegan Paul.

TOBIN, D., PEARSON, N., WILLAN, S. and SEDDON, N. (1981). 'Early maths and physical handicap', *Special Education: Forward Trends*, 8, 3, 36 – 39.

TOMLINSON, S. (1981a). *Educational Subnormality: a Study in Decision Making*. London: Routledge and Kegan Paul.

TOMLINSON, S. (1981b). 'Professional and ESN (M) education'. In: SWANN, W. (Ed) *The Practice of Special Education*. Oxford:Blackwell/Open University Press.

TOUGH, J. (1976). *Listening to Children Talking*. London: Schools Council/ Ward Lock.

WALL, W.D. (1979). *Constructive Education for Special Groups*. London: Harrap.

WARNOCK REPORT. GREAT BRITAIN. DEPARTMENT OF EDUCATION AND SCIENCE (1978). *Special Educational Needs*. London: HMSO.

WILSON, M.D. (1981). *The Curriculum in Special Schools*. London: Schools Council.

YOUNGHUSBAND, E., BIRCHALL, D., DAVIE, R. and PRINGLE, M.L.K. (Eds) (1970). *Living with Handicap*. London: National Children's Bureau.

Index